W9-AAS-072

Advance praise for
Reading Legitimation Crisis *in Tehran*:

"The importance of Postel's book reaches far
beyond a mere exercise in intellectual history. The
temptation is either to castigate Iran as a state run
by dangerous fundamentalist fanatics, or to cele-
brate it as a beacon of anti-imperialist resistance.
Both approaches miss the complexity of intellectual
and political life in Iran where, in a unique short-
circuit, political battles reverberate in the terms of
modern Western philosophy: some traditionalist
clerics refer to Heidegger, liberals to Habermas,
feminists to Arendt, some young "nihilists" to
deconstruction... The specter of an exotic country
is thus dispelled, and we can recognize in Iran our
own battles, fought more passionately than in our
own countries. This is Postel's great lesson: Iran's
story is our own."

—Slavoj Žižek

"A brilliant inquiry into the contemporary Iranian
predicament and what it means for the world. At a
time when all too many of our leading thinkers are
mired in the weeds of provincialism and narrow
ideological wars, Postel has written a work of grace,
intelligence, and towering integrity. *Reading*
Legitimation Crisis *in Tehran* is nothing less than a
masterpiece of moral and political criticism."

—Afshin Molavi, author of
The Soul of Iran: A Nation's Journey to Freedom

To Jean,
with regards.

Danny

11 January 2007

International House

Chicago

Reading *Legitimation Crisis*
in Tehran

Reading *Legitimation Crisis* in Tehran:
Iran and the Future of Liberalism

Danny Postel

PRICKLY PARADIGM PRESS
CHICAGO

Prickly Paradigm Press, LLC
5629 South University Avenue
Chicago, Il 60637

www.prickly-paradigm.com

ISBN: 0-9761475-7-2
LCCN: 2006936340

Printed in the United States of America on acid-free
paper.

...even in the midst of a battle in which one is unmistakably on one side against another, there should be criticism, because there must be critical consciousness if there are to be issues, problems, values, even lives to be fought for....

—Edward Said, *The World, the Text and the Critic*

Introduction

This pamphlet is about four overlapping themes: the widespread confusion on the western Left about Iran; why the school of political thought that resonates with and animates dissident intellectuals in Iran today is liberalism rather than Marxism; the tremendous vibrancy of the political and philosophical dialogue that has taken shape in Iran and what lessons we might draw from it about the future of internationalism and solidarity; and Michel Foucault's complex engagement with the Iranian Revolution and how, in retrospect, we might make sense of it.

Iran occupies center stage in an array of volatile and interrelated geopolitical dramas. The protracted international negotiations over Iran's nuclear program are but one of the dramas in play. Iran possesses, argues the BBC Middle East analyst Roger Hardy, five geopolitical cards above and beyond the nuclear one. It is, to one extent or another, a key player in Lebanon/Hezbollah; the Palestinian-Israeli conflict; the global political economy of oil; the politics of Shiite minority communities in the Persian Gulf; and the devolving situation in Iraq.

Looming over all of these dramas is the specter of a calamitous confrontation between Iran and the United States (and/or Israel). There is agreement across the political spectrum that the Lebanon crisis of July-August 2006 is, if not an outright proxy war, a prefiguration of a larger conflict between Tehran and Washington. Though it is of course impossible to know at present what form that conflict will take—whether, for example, the US will launch a military attack on Iran—there is a pervasive sense that Iran and the US are on a collision course. Every few weeks seem to produce a new Seymour Hersh investigation in *The New Yorker* reporting the designs of some faction in the Pentagon to bomb Iran. Talk of a simmering regional conflict abounds, described varyingly in terms of a "Big War," a "Long War," even the "beginning of World War III." The house organ of neoconservatism, *The Weekly Standard*, has openly called for attacking Iran.

My own view is that a military attack on Iran, though certainly not outside the realm of possibility (and certainly not beyond the wildest dreams of the neocons), is unlikely. The rhetoric of looming show-downs and enemies at the gates is pumped up by and serves the interests of both regimes. Posturing aside, Bush and Ahmadinejad are in fact involved in a symbiotic dance, a game of Schmittian shadowboxing, if you will, in which each needs the other as an enemy and feeds on the other's rhetoric. Washington's saber-rattling and fire-breathing provides Tehran's hardliners with "just the ammunition they need to bring the masses into line in terms of ideology, religion, and nationalism and to demand their solidarity with their country," as the Iranian journalist Bahman Nirumand puts it.

Let there be no mistake: we must be absolutely adamant in opposing military action of any kind against Iran. Among the strongest arguments that can be made against an attack is that Iran's dissidents and human rights activists—the very forces in whose name the neocons speciously claim to speak— are themselves against any such attack. It's difficult for antiwar activists in the West to make that case, however, if we don't know anything about Iranian dissidents and human rights activists—if we aren't tuned in to what they're saying, let alone have direct contact with them. The "Don't Attack Iran" message found on many a button and bumper sticker these days is key, but only a partial position: it says what we're against, but what are we for? What, absent the threat of US military intervention, would be the western Left's position on Iran?

Meanwhile, in Tehran...

Largely obscured by this flurry and under the radar of the daily headlines, an ominous development is underway: 2006 has seen a massive crackdown on dissent and a precipitous deterioration of the human rights situation in Iran. In what some are calling a "second Cultural Revolution" and an attempt to "reassert the values of 1979," intellectuals, trade unionists, and student movement leaders have been imprisoned; demonstrations have been violently crushed; newspapers have been closed; and human rights organizations have been banned.

The philosopher Ramin Jahanbegloo, one of Iran's most prominent intellectual figures, was arrested and placed in solitary confinement for four months. Without bringing any formal charges against him, the regime floated vague accusations of "contacts with foreigners" and fomenting a "soft" or "Velvet" revolution in Iran. (As a friend of mine has pointed out, the regime is apparently oblivious to the almost universally positive connotations of the Czechoslovak events which gave birth to that name and indeed unwittingly identifies itself with the loathsome system toppled in 1989.) As a condition of his release, Jahanbegloo was required to make a degrading "confession" of his "crimes." (Chapter Four of this volume consists of a dialogue with Jahanbegloo I conducted shortly before his arrest.)

On May Day in Tehran a rally of bus drivers was smashed by police and security forces, who arrested more than ten union members and students who had joined them. The rally had been called to demand the reinstatement of nearly 200 union members who had been sacked following a strike in January, and also to demand the release of the union's imprisoned leader, Mansour Osanloo.

In June, in Tehran, a peaceful sit-in for women's rights was immediately broken up by police, who pepper sprayed and beat participants with clubs. A former student leader and ex-member of parliament, Ali Akbar Mousavi Khoeni, was arrested amidst the breakup and has been behind bars ever since.

In July, the student leader Akbar Mohammadi died in prison while on a hunger strike to protest his treatment (specifically his lack of access to medical care); his family believes that the severe beatings to which he was subjected led to his death. Another student leader, Ahmad Batebi, who had been out of prison briefly, was re-arrested and taken to an undisclosed location, where he is believed to be on a hunger strike.

In August, the organization headed by the human rights lawyer and Nobel Peace laureate Shirin Ebadi, the Defenders of Human Rights Center, was banned, leading Ebadi to issue an urgent appeal to human rights supporters around the world to be on alert and warning that her own arrest could be imminent. In September, Ahmadinejad announced a purge of "liberal" and "secular" instructors from Iran's universities and the government's Press Supervisory Board shut down the country's leading reform-oriented newspaper, *Shargh*, along with three other publications.

These developments are not unrelated to one another. An acute foreboding pervades Iran's intellectual and cultural landscape today. "Censorship of literature and the press, filtering of websites, the confiscation of satellite dishes and censorship of film and theater are mounting day by day," declares the Iranian Writers Association. The Ahmadinejad government is establishing a climate of fear, rolling back the opening created during the reform period of 1997-2005 and redrawing the boundaries of public space in Iran. "[A]nything that even hints at renewal, openness and diversity" faces censure, Bahman Nirumand observes.

Commenting on the June women's rights demonstration, the Iranian feminist Golbarg Bashi wrote that the Ahmadinejad government

> appears far more intolerant of such grassroots movements, which might indeed snowball to question the very constitutional foundation of the Islamic Republic... The brutality and immediacy with which [the demonstration] was ruthlessly crushed... speak of the increasing anxiety of the Islamic Republic about its prolonged legitimacy.

Indeed I contend that what we are witnessing in Iran today is precisely what Jürgen Habermas, in his felicitously titled 1975 book, termed a legitimation crisis. A legitimation crisis occurs, in the words of the philosopher Thomas McCarthy, "when the 'organizational principle' of a society does not permit the resolution of problems that are critical for its continued existence." (I quote McCarthy, who translated

Legitimation Crisis, rather than Habermas himself, as the former's prose style is, shall we say, more musical than that of the master.) Every day it becomes more evident that the "organizational principle" of the Islamic Republic indeed fails to "permit the resolution of problems that are critical for its continued existence." What else are Ahmadinejad's widespread crackdown and ideological maneuvers if not a desperate attempt to legitimate the Islamic Republic in the face of a civil society that has outgrown its strictures and passionately craves change?

Herein lay the other half of the Habermasian equation. "[C]risis tendencies," notes McCarthy, are "pregnant with the future": the "seeds of the new society are being formed in the womb of the old." Echoing this insight, Shadi Vatanparast, a promoter of underground music in Tehran, likens developments in Iran today to a chick bursting from an eggshell: "People are pushing from inside. [The shell] is getting thinner and thinner."

But this pamphlet is titled *Reading* Legitimation Crisis *in Tehran*, not *Legitimation Crisis in Tehran*. Though the latter would certainly be worth writing, what I'm undertaking here is not a Habermasian analysis of present-day Iran but rather a meditation on why—and how—thinkers like Habermas, Hannah Arendt, Isaiah Berlin, and Karl Popper are read by Iranian intellectuals today and what their ideas look like when refracted back to us through that Persian prism. "Our dilemma," the Iranian political theorist Javad Tabataba'i has said, "is how to understand the gap that has developed

between us and the West since the Renaissance."
"[W]e need to re-link to this part of our tradition that
also inspired the West." "We can re-read [the great
medieval Islamic philosopher-scientist] ibn-Sina
[Avrceina]," for example, "with a Western horizon in
mind." What I propose is the mirror image of
Tabataba'i's proposal: that we in the West should "re-
link" to the thinkers in our tradition who have
inspired Iran, and thus re-read Habermas and Berlin
with a Persian horizon in mind. (In Chapter Three I
try to show what that might look like.)

Readers will, I hope, forgive me for my simultaneously obscure and coy title. It is a play on the
titles of two books: the aforementioned *Legitimation
Crisis* and Azar Nafisi's widely-read 2003 memoir
Reading Lolita in Tehran, which I discuss in Chapter
Two. I chose my title in order to evoke both the actual
legitimation crisis and the intellectual ferment taking
place in Iran today. While Nafisi's book movingly
explores that ferment from a literary angle, my focus is
on Iran's philosophical-political profile (to borrow
another Habermasianism): it is about the fascinating
reception of thinkers like Habermas, Arendt, and
Berlin among Iranians today.

Moment of Decision

We are at a pivotal moment, not only in the geopolitical sense but in terms of how we are to make sense of
and relate to what's happening both politically and

intellectually inside Iran today. There is an extraordinary intellectual upheaval taking place in Iran, what Jahanbegloo calls a "renaissance of liberalism" (explored in some detail in Chapters Two and Four). Most western leftists are not merely unaware of this phenomenon but, more to the point and for reasons I attempt to explain in this volume, they're stuck in interpretive frameworks that blind them to its contours. Amidst the wave of repression currently convulsing the country, moreover, Iranian dissidents and human rights activists are actively seeking support for their embattled struggles—not, as I'll discuss in a moment, the support of western governments, but of intellectuals, writers, and NGOs. That is to say, from us. There is an astounding degree of confusion over this extremely elementary but vital distinction among large swaths of the western Left. And it is a confusion with very real consequences.

Thus in the summer and fall of 2006, Akbar Ganji, Iran's preeminent dissident, traveled to Europe and North America to raise awareness of the human rights situation back home and to seek support for the democratic struggle that his own story has in many ways come to represent. Ganji had spent the first half of the decade as a political prisoner, locked in solitary confinement inside Tehran's notorious Evin prison. Possessing intimate knowledge, from his own treatment, of the conditions Iran's dissidents routinely face in prison, he decided to hold a three-day hunger strike in front of the United Nations in solidarity with three particular Iranian political prisoners, each symbolizing the plights of distinct fronts in the

Iranian struggle: the aforementioned trade unionist Mansour Osanloo; the philosopher Ramin Jahanbegloo; and the former student leader and ex-parliamentarian Ali Akbar Mousavi Khoeni. In coordination with Ganji's action, parallel hunger strikes were held in cities around the world, from Toronto and Paris to Stockholm and Berlin.

While abroad, Ganji also delivered a series of talks at universities and to groups like Amnesty International and PEN, and met one-on-one with several intellectuals. Significantly, and to Ganji's great credit, he declined invitations to meet with heads of state (including one from the White House), explaining that he sought the support of NGOs, civil society, and intellectuals, not governments. He veered clear of the corridors of power and made himself useless to the neoconservatives who fancy themselves the esteemed allies of Iranian democrats (this while they go to bat for a Stalinist-Islamist cult group once funded by Saddam Hussein and officially deemed a terrorist organization by the State Department—yes, you heard that right—called the Mujahedin-e Khalq [MEK]).

But if Ganji shunned the neoconservatives, he was—with one important exception—no more eager to cross-pollinate with the West's radical intelligentsia. Which intellectuals Ganji chose as interlocutors on his tour is highly illuminating—and goes to the heart of this volume's argument.

It's no accident that in Germany he made a point of meeting with Habermas, whose influence in Iranian dissident and intellectual circles is towering, probably greater than that of any other living thinker.

(This is due in no small measure to the philosopher's 2002 visit to Iran, discussed in Chapters Two and Four.) While in Germany he also met with Shmuel Eisenstadt, the theorist of "multiple modernities." (The theme of modernity—*tajadod* in Persian—looms large in Iranian intellectual life. It's striking how often it pops up not only in the theoretical literature but more broadly in public discourse.)

In London he sought out neither Tariq Ali nor George Galloway; rather, he met with the liberal internationalists Mary Kaldor and David Held of the London School of Economics and the social theorist and former LSE Director, Anthony Giddens. As it happens, Held's book *Models of Democracy*—hardly part of the left cannon—has been translated into Persian and is widely read by Iranian intellectuals and journalists. Giddens is of course held in near universal contempt on the Left for his writings on the "Third Way" and his role as court intellectual for Tony Blair, but his work on modernity enjoys a sizable readership in Iran.

In Canada, Ganji sought out Charles Taylor, another philosopher to whose writings one finds references sprinkled throughout contemporary Iranian thought and whose politics belong decidedly in the democratic-pluralist rather than the Marxist camp.

In the US, Ganji met with Richard Rorty, who has also lectured in Iran and enjoys a following there (discussed in Chapter Four). Rorty once playfully described his own politics as a kind of "postmodern bourgeois liberalism"; he is a Deweyan, *Dissent* magazine-style social democrat, solidly on the left of the

American political schemata but considered hopelessly tepid by most self-styled radicals. Ganji also met with the sociologist Robert Bellah and with the philosopher Martha Nussbaum.

The other American thinker with whom Ganji met—and the only unambiguous radical—was Noam Chomsky. In one sense it was a peculiar choice, since liberalism tends to speak more to Iranian intellectuals than does radicalism. And yet Chomsky is personally held in high regard among many Iranian intellectuals (as Ramin Jahanbegloo explains in our dialogue in Chapter Four). Chomsky was admonished by numerous radicals not to meet with Ganji, on the grounds that the Iranian dissident was insufficiently critical of neoliberalism and US imperialism. (In Chapters One and Two I discuss the disconnect and political tunnel vision in this sort of thinking.)

To his great credit, Chomsky ignored those admonitions and engaged in what Fred Halliday calls "critical solidarity" with Ganji. He not only asked his fellow dissident what we—western supporters of the democratic struggle in Iran—can do to help (an absolutely vital gesture—one that virtually no one else on the Left has made, as I discuss in Chapter One); he went further, suggesting to Ganji that he formulate a more concrete program outlining the Iranian democratic movement's goals and how it proposes to go about realizing them. Ganji took up the idea and the two men agreed to continue the dialogue.

I have my disagreements with Chomsky, but to my mind this was an exemplary political moment, an expression of exactly the kind of critical solidarity so sorely lacking on both the liberal *and* the radical Left today. Precious few leftists today have more than a vague clue who Ganji even is. Go to the websites of *The Nation*, *In These Times*, *The Progressive*, and *New Left Review* and search for his name—see how many times he is even mentioned, let alone how many profiles of him or essays on him appear. Thus the leading dissident figure in a country at the center of the geopolitical action is effectively off the radar of the Left.

How are we to make sense of this state of affairs?

To be fair, if you go to the website of the Marxist magazine *Monthly Review*, you will find Ganji discussed—in a smear job attacking him for having insufficient anti-capitalist credentials. (At least they can't be accused of ignoring him!) But to be really fair, Amy Goodman had Ganji on her widely listened-to radio show *Democracy Now!* and did quite a good interview with him. I admit to being surprised by this (albeit pleasantly so) for two reasons. First because Goodman, like most American leftists, views Iran largely through an American prism—the prism of American imperialism, which is no less an American prism for being critical, as opposed to uncritical, of US foreign policy. Anti-imperialism can become a form, if an inverted one, of imperialism: for both, it's all about the US. Likewise, anti-Orientalism can turn into a form of Orientalism, as Janet Afary and Kevin Anderson argue it did for Foucault in his encounter with the Iranian Revolution (an episode I discuss in Chapter Three). But the more proximate cause for

my surprise was that when Goodman interviewed
Shirin Ebadi in June of 2004 she was exclusively
interested in the latter's criticisms of US foreign
policy (Washington's support for Saddam Hussein
during the Iran-Iraq War, for instance) while side-
stepping Ebadi's thoughts on the internal political
situation in Iran.

    In this same vein, consider the following.
Ebadi went on a speaking tour in the spring of 2006
to discuss her recently-published autobiography, *Iran
Awakening*. As someone who every day of every week
defends the victims of the regime's brutal abuses—
indeed as someone who has done jail time for engaging in that work—the issue of the Islamic Republic's
human rights practices tends to feature rather
centrally in her scheme of things. Which is not to say
that it's the only issue on her agenda, or that it in any
way blunts her criticisms of the United States and its
foreign policy—quite the contrary. She has spoken
out in no uncertain terms against the Iraq War, the
detainee base at Guantánamo, and the torture
inflicted by US soldiers at Abu Ghraib—and has
made it utterly clear that she opposes any US intervention in Iran. And yet, at a public event for her
book in London, an antiwar activist instructed her
that she should not denounce Iran's human rights
record—indeed not discuss it at all—explaining that
doing so only plays into the hands of the warmongers
and fuels the fires of imperialism. Ebadi upbraided
her would-be sage in the strongest possible terms.
Leaning over the lectern and waving her finger at the
activist, she made plain that any antiwar movement

that advocates silence in the face of tyranny, for whatever reason, can count her out.

This pamphlet is an attempt to diagnose the mindset of that antiwar activist and the many others on the Left who are conflicted and flummoxed over Iran. It is, as well, an attempt to explain why Ganji and other Iranian dissidents gravitate toward liberal rather than radical-leftist intellectuals, and what lessons there might be in this about how to think about Iran today. It is an attempt to understand why in his essays and speeches Ganji invokes the figures of Kant, Mill, and Camus while criticizing those of Marx, Sartre, and Marcuse. Lest I in any way leave the impression that I am an uncritical champion of Actually Existing Liberalism, however, a substantial section of Chapter Two is devoted to a critical appraisal of what I see as liberalism's shortcomings and inadequacies.

It is critical that we think through these questions—not only because of the pressing situation Iran faces today externally as well as internally, but because of their relevance for the progressive project itself.

Danny Postel
September 2006
Chicago

CHAPTER ONE

Why So Many Leftists are Flummoxed About Iran: We Know What We're Against, But What Are We For?

In June 2003, at the height of the student-led protests against the Iranian government, the conservative journalist Andrew Sullivan conducted a little test. He scanned the left-wing media and the blogosphere to see what kind of coverage the unrest was getting. He found that *Indymedia*, a highly trafficked forum for progressive activists, hadn't a word. He took a look at other left-wing publications—same results. He then quoted a first-hand account of the protests by an Iranian student organizer:

> It has become almost routine for us to go out at night, chant slogans, get beaten, lose some of our friends, see our sisters beaten, and then return home. Each night we set to the streets only to be swept away the next dawn by agents of the regime. Two nights ago, on Amirabad Street, we wrote "Down with Khomeini" on the ground. Before long, the mullah's vigilantes attacked us on their motorcycles. They struck a female student before my eyes so harshly that she was no longer able to walk. As she fell to the ground, four members of Ansaar-e-Hezbollah surrounded her, kicking her. When I and two other students threw stones at them so that they would leave her alone, they threatened us. We escaped into a lane and hid in a house whose owner, an old lady, had left the door open for us. A few minutes later, we saw the young lady being carried away by riot police, her feet dragging on the ground, her shattered teeth hanging out of her stillbleeding mouth. At least three of my best friends have been detained; nobody knows anything about their fate.

Where did Sullivan find this report? Not on *ZNet* or *Commondreams.org* or *AlterNet* or *TomPaine.com*, it turned out—but on the website of the right-wing *National Review*. One would think, Sullivan wrote in *Salon*, that the demonstrations in the streets of Tehran would be big news in the left press. You've got a "grass-roots, student-run, anti-theocracy movement" reaching "some sort of critical mass," he wrote. And, quoting a blogger by the name of Don Watkins, "here are a bunch of brave souls fighting a tyrannical regime through the old liberal favorite of massive protests." And yet, virtually no reaction from US progressives.

How to explain this "shocking silence," as Sullivan deemed it? Another blogger, Matthew Yglesias, "let it slip," Sullivan enthused, that "these stories about the Iranian student movement have been so relentless[ly] hyped on rightwing sites that I think we on the left have been shying away from the story."

Sullivan's own interpretation:

> Much of the antiwar left has sadly long since stopped caring about the actual freedom of people under oppressive regimes, except, of course, if their plight is a way to blame or excoriate the United States.... Could anyone on the left actually sympathize with the sexist, homophobic, anti-Semitic theocrats in Tehran? Of course not. But it seems that many of them hate the American right more than they hate foreign tyranny.

In an important article in the magazine *Foreign Policy in Focus*, veteran leftist Jeremy Brecher echoed Sullivan's argument. "Normally," he wrote, "the global peace movement and political left would respond to repression by an authoritarian, theocratic regime with outrage and protest. But so far there has been a deafening silence." But Brecher disagrees with Sullivan's explanation for the Left's silence; instead, Brecher suggests that "there is wariness about intervening in a complex, multiplayer drama in which the left could have an impact contrary to what it intends."

I'm going to return to this question of why American progressives have by and large been silent about the situation in Iran today—a condition • captured poignantly by Janet Afary, an Iranian feminist and historian, who describes the "sideways glances" she gets from American leftists when she speaks in support of the progressive movement in Iran. First, I want to draw out the comparison, which I think is an instructive one, between US solidarity activism around Central America in the 1980s and the conspicuous lack of activism around Iran today.

How many American progressives (not including Iranians and Iranian-Americans) knew who Shirin Ebadi was before she was awarded the Nobel Peace Prize in October? Almost no one, I think it's fair to say. By the same token, how many of us knew who Rigoberta Menchú was before she won the prize in 1992? Many, if not most of us; we'd seen her speak, read her autobiography, or had simply come to know her story by osmosis in activist circles. Why this difference? Why hadn't more of us heard the name Shirin Ebadi?

Consider the number of Central America solidarity groups that have come onto the scene over the years: CISPES (the Committee in Solidarity with the People of El Salvador); the Nicaragua Solidarity Committee; OSGUA (the Organization in Solidarity with Guatemala); Witness for Peace; Pledge of Resistance; Women for Guatemala; and on and on. How many American progressives, at one point or another between 1980 and the signing of the Guatemalan peace accords in 1996, were involved, at one level or another, in solidarity work around Central America? Tons of us.

How many of us, in contrast, have ever had any engagement with Iran solidarity work? Or even read a book about the current situation in Iran? I'm not talking about a book like Stephen Kinzer's *All the Shah's Men: An American Coup and the Roots of Middle East Terror*, about the US-engineered 1953 coup, enormously valuable though such books are. I mean a book about the internal political situation in Iran today, a book, say, like Reza Afshari's *Human Rights in Iran*. (Shamefully—though revealingly—Afshari's extraordinary book has gone almost completely ignored by left-wing academics and journalists. Do a search and see how many reviews of it come up.)

Christine List's 1995 documentary film *No Nos Tientes* ("Don't Tempt Us") vibrantly portrayed the struggle of the Guatemalan student movement. The images in that film—of university students demonstrating nonviolently against a repressive and murderous regime, risking their lives in the process, many of them taking unspeakable beatings, others tortured, some killed—radiated off the screen and stirred many American activists. When I hear and think about student demonstrations, those images come to mind for me.

Flash forward to Tehran in June 2003. Government vigilantes storm student dormitories wielding clubs and thrashing students with chains. They toss one student out a window to his death. On the streets, helicopters hover overhead, elite units of antiriot police gather, and Intelligence Ministry agents

buzz around on motorbikes. Plainclothes security offi-
cers detain student radicals at gunpoint and shove
them into cars. Students are beaten and tortured in jail.

Whereas American leftists went to Guatemala
to support the student radicals, wrote about them,
made films about them, raised money for them, and
brought them on speaking tours of the US to spread
the word about their struggle, no such luck for their
counterparts in Iran.

Back to Sullivan and Brecher. I agree with
Brecher's point that the situation in Iran is "a complex,
multiplayer drama." This also describes the situation in
Bosnia in the 1990s, for that matter, which was another
conflict most leftists—with a handful of noteworthy
exceptions—sat out. Compared to Central America in
the 1980s, Bosnia in the 1990s and Iran today do
appear somewhat perplexing. They don't lend themselves nearly as well to the kind of analytical prism
through which we on the Left made sense, for example, of El Salvador, Nicaragua, or Guatemala during
the high tide of our solidarity activism, the Reagan
years. In Central America, there was precious little in
the form of ambiguity or complexity. You had military
juntas and death squads, in concert with essentially
feudal elites and corporate oligarchs, running the show
with the active support of the United States. In a
nutshell, a bloodbath of imperial domination, rapacious
exploitation, scorched earth terror and mass murder—
in which the United States was complicit from top to
bottom.

The victims of this carnival of atrocities were
on the receiving end of imperial power. Our solidarity

with them was a direct extension of our opposition to the Empire and its ravages.

What happens, though, when people are struggling against tyranny and repression, but the tyranny and repression are not being perpetrated by the Empire or its proxies—not only not perpetrated by the Empire or its proxies, but, to take the case of Iran today, the regime in question is a sworn enemy of the US Empire?

Despite his disagreement with Sullivan about why the Left has been largely silent on Iran, Brecher realizes that some things are true even if Andrew Sullivan says they are. "It is always a temptation for the peace movement and the left to soft-pedal our critique of regimes," Brecher writes, when those regimes are official enemies of the United States. "It is particularly hard to find a balanced position," he argues, when Washington has demonized the government against which the students are agitating, branding it as part of an "axis of evil." This casts a blinding light on things, embedding them in "a context of geopolitical manipulation that complicates the picture."

Let's face it: it's just plain uncomfortable for leftists to say anything that sounds like it could also come out of the mouth of George Bush or Paul Wolfowitz.

And yet, Brecher argues, "failure to defend human rights in such circumstances only plays into the hands of the Bush juggernaut." Progressives must, he contends, be known as "people whose fundamental solidarity" is with "all people who are struggling for liberation from oppression."

I agree with this wholeheartedly. We should not allow Washington's rhetoric to have a silencing effect on us. To do so is to let Bush and the neocons do our thinking for us. We should express solidarity with our Iranian comrades regardless of the Empire's pronouncements.

And rather than accept those pronouncements at face value, why not unmask them for the opportunistic propaganda they are? Why not point out that despite their rhetoric, the Bush administration couldn't care less about democracy and human rights? Whatever the administration says about supporting the student reformers, the reality is, as Brecher puts it, that it sees Iran as "a critical source of oil and a powerful country that currently threatens—but could support—both US and Israeli interests." "Encouraging the student revolt," he points out, "is done in the interest of Washington's agenda, which cannot be accurately described as seeking freedom, independence, and self-determination for the people of Iran," but are, rather, about "oil deals and a cooperative stance regarding Iraq."

We have to distinguish our progressive criticisms of the Islamic republic, in other words, from Washington's hollow and self-serving ones.

The picture gets further complicated, and the Left gets further flummoxed, over the role of Empire in the Iranian context. The memory of the 1953 coup burns furiously in the minds of many Iranians to this day. Because anti-imperialism is our primary conceptual organizing principle, leftists are of course highly attuned to such sentiments. Particularly in this era of

Empire fever and regime-change mania, we reflexively and viscerally oppose US interference in other countries—and understandably so. Anti-imperialist pronouncements coming out of Iran thus have a certain resonance for many leftists. The supreme cleric Ayatollah Ali Khamenei has characterized the students as "American mercenaries." As the Middle East scholar Juan Cole points out, that kind of accusation "has resonance in a country where US conspiracies to change the government—like the 1953 CIA coup—have actually succeeded." (It should be recalled, however, that the Islamists deploy the 1953 coup in bad faith: not only did they oppose Iranian president Mohammad Mossadegh for his secularism and liberalism; they even had their own plans to take him out. And after taking power in 1979, they obliterated the Mossadeghi National Front Party. This little footnote has largely been forgotten but is hugely relevant to the present situation.)

The problem is that denunciations of US Empire in Iran today are the rhetorical dominion of the Right, not the Left. It is the reactionary clergy, not the students, who wield the idiom of anti-imperialism. Regime hard-liners "legitimate their suppression of the students," Brecher points out, "as necessary to guard against 'foreign forces'"; the mullahs denounced the awarding of the Nobel Prize to Shirin Ebadi as "the result of the cultural hegemony of western civilization," a tool "intended to serve the interests of colonialism and the decadent world." This kind of talk can run an interference pattern on the ideological compasses of many leftists.

In contrast, for students, feminists, human rights activists, and dissidents agitating for pluralism and democracy in Iran today, opposition to US imperialism is not the central issue. The student movement's principal demand, as Brecher notes, is "to eliminate the power of the self-perpetuating theocratic elite" over the Iranian state. A simple stance of "hands off Iran," end of discussion, is not what those struggling for change in Iran need from progressives around the world. Of course we should be steadfast in opposing any US military intervention in Iran—that's the easy part. But it's not the end of the discussion. Iran is, as the Iranian anthropologist Ziba Mir-Hosseini puts it, "a state at war with itself." Progressives everywhere should take sides in that war and actively support the forces of democracy, feminism, pluralism, human rights, and freedom of expression.

It's not that the students and other reformers in Iran are pro-imperialist. Quite the contrary. Ebadi, for example, has made it perfectly clear that she opposes US military intervention, advocating instead a nonviolent, internal transformation of Iranian society. But US imperialism is simply not the central issue for them—and this, I think, is a stumbling block for many American leftists, because it is the central issue for us. We're better at making sense of situations in which the US Empire is the foe and building our solidarity with other people around that. That was the case in Guatemala—as it was in Indochina, Chile, El Salvador, Nicaragua, and East Timor.

But that model simply doesn't apply to situations in which the struggles of oppressed groups are not aimed directly against American imperialism. And that's a serious blind spot. It creates myopia on the part of American leftists. Anti-imperialism can turn into a kind of tunnel vision, its own form of fundamentalism. Cases that fall outside its scheme simply get left out, and our solidarity with struggles around the world is determined by George Bush, rather than by our principles.

This is a betrayal of the great radical tradition of internationalism. Think of the thousands of leftists from around the world who went to fight in the Spanish civil war. By the logic of today's anti-imperialist Left, that cause might not rank very high on a list of political priorities. After all, it wasn't a struggle against US imperialism. In fact, it wasn't a struggle against imperialism at all. It was a struggle against fascism—and in the spirit of international solidarity, myriad leftists went to fight in that struggle. Indeed, many died in it. (Lest I over-romanticize the brigades, of course I realize that many of them were Stalinist. Let me be clear that my sympathy belongs with the anarchist and independent socialist forces that fought in Spain, not with the Stalinists. But my argument is more about the underlying spirit that guided the solidarity than the particular doctrines of the groups in question.)

I'd like to suggest that revisiting that idea—the principle of solidarity with people struggling against oppression everywhere, whoever their oppressors are, the vision that inspired the international brigades that went to defend the Spanish Republic—would do the Left a world of good today.

Am I arguing that the left shouldn't be anti-imperialist? Absolutely not. I'm arguing that opposition to US empire is necessary, but not sufficient. It's crucial—especially in this time of US hegemony. But it's not enough, and when it becomes an all-consuming paradigm, it blinds rather than guides.

To be concrete, and to end on a positive note, I'd like to spell out what I think solidarity with our Iranian comrades might involve. To quote Brecher yet again:

> The goal for the global antiwar movement and the left should be a nonviolent transition to democracy in Iran complete with human rights and freedom from domination by outside powers.... The first step toward this goal is to demand that the Iranian regime release all political prisoners, regardless of their beliefs, and end the suppression of protesters' human rights by its own agencies and those of vigilante groups.... More direct contact, ranging from solidarity delegations to the kind of volunteer human rights observation and nonviolent intervention provided by the "Internationals" in Palestine, would be difficult but appropriate. So would a campaign for international human rights monitors.

Another thing, it seems to me, would be to bring Iranian activists to North America on speaking tours, to raise awareness and resources for the movement there, to help it get more exposure in the western press, and to build the kinds of personal bridges that those of us who've been involved in solidarity work over the years know are so essential.

One barrier we face is that few of us on the American left speak Persian or have ever been to Iran. Solidarity work with Central America was naturally made easier by the fact that Spanish is the unofficial second language of this country—it's taught in virtually every school; traveling to Central America is less of a voyage than traveling to Iran; and the Central American community in this country is much bigger than the Iranian one, creating more points of contact. But these obstacles can be overcome with the right amount of will. Despite even greater chasms, large numbers of progressives mobilized around East Timor's struggle for independence from Indonesia.

A key, I think, is to generate more dialogue about the situation in Iran. The role of Iranians living here is fundamental. American progressives have an enormous amount to learn about Iran. Just as dialogue and close collaboration between Central Americans living in the United States and American activists was of the essence in the Central America solidarity movement, these kinds of connections need to be developed vis-à-vis Iran. We need to make contact with Iranian students and human rights activists and ask them what they need from us, thus beginning to build the kinds of relationships that were so vital in sustaining solidarity struggles of the past.

CHAPTER TWO

What Iranian Liberalism Can Teach the West

In her 2003 memoir *Reading Lolita in Tehran* (much maligned, and unfairly so, in my view), the Iranian literary scholar Azar Nafisi tells the story of a group of her female students who surreptitiously gathered in her living room once a week to discuss works of western literature deemed unfit for classroom instruction by the Islamic Republic's censors. Over a period of close to two years in the mid-1990s, the women snuck into their teacher's home every Thursday morning, removed the veils they are legally required to wear in public, and mixed it up over Nabokov, Fitzgerald,

Flaubert, Jane Austen, Henry James, and Saul Bellow. *Reading Lolita* is about how these women experienced internal freedom amidst external repression—about a struggle to carve out a space for the imagination under the crushing weight of a regime committed to administering the totality of public and private life alike. It's a story about the transformative power of great literature, its ability to connect and transport its readers to an outside world—in this case, a world that is prohibited, closed, off limits. It's an attempt to contravene, however momentarily and precariously, what Andrei Codrescu calls "the disappearance of the outside."

As Nafisi shows, the encounter with books under such conditions has a transformative effect not only on those who read them, but on the works themselves. The women in Nafisi's clandestine book club see things in these novels that people on the outside are unlikely to see. Nabokov's *Invitation to a Beheading* resonates differently for readers in the Islamic Republic of Iran from the way it does for readers, say, in North America or Western Europe.

Indeed, a confidant of Nafisi's, a reclusive intellectual she calls her "magician," tells her that she "will not be able to write about Austen without writing about us, about this place where you rediscovered Austen." "The Austen you know is so irretrievably linked to this place, this land and these trees," he professes, that Nafisi can't think this is the same Austen she read in graduate school in the West. "This is the Austen you read here, in a place where the film censor is nearly blind and where they hang people in the streets and put a curtain across the sea to segregate men and women."

In turn, I think it's fair to say that we in the West can discover a great deal about our own literature by seeing it reflected back through the prism of an outsider's perspective or interpretation. We can gain new insights and discover fresh angles on the works read in Nafisi's group by seeing those works refracted through the prism of the Iranians whose imaginations were kindled and whose lives were transformed by them.

If you've read reviews of *Reading Lolita in Tehran* or had conversations with friends about it, you know that almost invariably people comment on how it makes them think anew about novels they'd never thought about in quite those ways, and how the discussions in Nafisi's group cast new light on canonical European and American authors they'd grown bored with. (Many have resolved to finally read some of those novels for the first time in their lives.) In an interview, Nafisi poignantly captures this two-way street—this process of give-and-take. The West's "gifts to us," she explains, "have been *Lolita* and *Gatsby*," while Iran's gift to the West "has been reasserting those values that they now take for granted..." It is one, she says, of "reminding" us. My contention here is that this insight can be applied to international politics.

If you want to go where people are reading Hannah Arendt and Karl Popper, Nafisi has admonished, "go to Iran." Go to Iran, I would add, if you want to go where people are reading Jürgen

Habermas, Isaiah Berlin, Leszek Kolakowski, and Immanuel Kant. "There have been more translations of Kant into Persian in the past decade," Vali Nasr reports, "than into any other language, and these have gone into multiple printings." Abdollah Momeni, the leader of Iran's most prominent student-activist group (Daftar-e Tahkim-e Vahdat), claims Habermas as his chief inspiration. The speeches and writings of Akbar Ganji, Iran's leading dissident, are peppered with references to Kant, John Stuart Mill, and Albert Camus.

Indeed, there are often "more vibrant resonances of 'Continental' thought" in places like Iran, notes the political philosopher Fred Dallmayr, "than can be found in Europe today." In a rich elaboration on this point, he observes:

> This does not mean that European perspectives are simply disseminated across the world without reciprocity or reciprocal learning. Nor does it mean that local origins are simply erased in favor of a bland universalism.... What it does mean is that landscapes and localities undergo symbolic metamorphoses, and that experiences once localized at a given place increasingly find echoes or resonance chambers among distant societies and peoples.

One would be hard pressed to find a more luminous illustration of Dallmayr's point than contemporary Iran. In the words of the Iranian scholar Farideh Farhi, there is an

> elaborate and extremely rich conversation that has taken shape in Iran in the past few years concern-

ing the requirements of a democratic and transparent political system and the relationship between faith and freedom.

The Iranian political scientist Mehrdad Mashayekhi describes "an epoch-making renaissance in [Iran's] political culture and discourse." The Tehran-based philosopher Ramin Jahanbegloo (interviewed in Chapter Four) argues that there is nothing less than "a renaissance of liberalism" taking place in Iran today. (Indeed Jahanbegloo's own work perfectly embodies the intellectual conversation between Iran and the West. In addition to his books of conversations, in English, with Isaiah Berlin and Ashis Nandy and, in French, George Steiner, he has written books, in Persian, on Machiavelli, Kant, Hegel, Schopenhauer, and Tagore and, in French, Gandhi. As well, he has brought an endless stream of Western intellectuals to lecture in Iran in recent years, among them Nandy, Fred Dallmayr, Richard Rorty, Agnes Heller, Antonio Negri, Michael Ignatieff, and Timothy Garton Ash.) Why is there such an intense interest in these authors in Iran today? How do books like *The Open Society and Its Enemies* and *The Origins of Totalitarianism* speak to contemporary Iranians? Do the ideas of Habermas and Berlin look the same to Iranian intellectuals and dissidents as they do to us? And of the many intellectual-political currents emanating from the West today—Marxism, poststructuralism, postcolonialism, subaltern studies, and various blends thereof—why is liberalism the most popular school of thought among Iranian intellectuals and students at this historical moment?

First, let me state exactly what I mean by liberalism. There is of course a robust and complex theoretical debate among philosophers, political theorists, and intellectual historians about the precise contours and varieties of liberal thought, its historical evolution, its tensions and contradictions, and the like.

Many of the arguments being advanced in that debate are important and useful. But for purposes of this essay, I'm going to focus very concretely on what liberalism means in Iran today. Broadly speaking, it means the struggle for human rights, women's rights, civil liberties, pluralism, religious toleration, freedom of expression, and multiparty democracy.

The struggle for these things defines the upheaval in Iran today. And the reason is pretty straightforward: Iran is a theocratic police state. The so-called Islamic Republic, established after the 1979 Iranian Revolution, defines itself largely in opposition to these things. Its human rights record is atrocious. Newspapers and magazines that criticize the regime are routinely shut down. Dissident journalists and intellectuals are jailed and tortured, in many cases killed. Article 4 of Iran's Constitution prohibits the establishment of any law or policy not in keeping with Islam. Without the official permission of the Ministry of Islamic Culture and Guidance, in the words of the Iranian writer Naghmeh Zarbafian, "no books or magazines are published, no audiotapes are distributed, no movies are shown, and no cultural organization is established." The unelected Guardian

Council—a body of six clerics appointed by the unelected Supreme Leader—has the authority to veto any legislation passed by Iran's parliament and decides who may or may not stand for office. Women are required to follow a strict dress code, covering their heads in public. A 16-year-old girl was recently sentenced to death and hung for having sex outside of marriage. That she claimed to have been raped counted for nothing.

Under conditions like these, liberalism is a radical political project. A triumphant Iranian liberalism would involve dismantling the entire apparatus of the reigning political order and constructing a dramatically different one. In the Iranian context, liberalism is a matter of life and death: people are literally putting their lives on the line when they write articles for opposition newspapers calling for an end to theocratic rule; when they take to the streets to participate in student demonstrations for democracy; when they publish a blog at an Internet café that dares to criticize the regime's human rights record.

Things, in other words, that most of us in western liberal democracies, for all their faults, are at liberty to do without worrying about getting that knock at the door in the middle of the night; without fearing that one of our relatives will suddenly disappear; without fearing that much of anything will happen to us, let alone that we will be tortured or killed. We can take these freedoms pretty much for granted, and pretty much do.

Iranians don't, because they can't. For them, liberalism is a fighting faith. They have to struggle, at great personal risk, to realize the "bourgeois liberties" we take for granted. "Human rights and freedom are luxuries for us," says Akbar Ganji. "In order to get them, we have to pay. We have to fight, actively resist, go to jail."

As the French political philosopher Pierre Manent says, most of us who live in liberal democracies have forgotten what it means to be political. We are tempted, he writes, "to forget that [we] are political animals." We're largely incognizant of the struggles that had to be waged in order to achieve the rights and arrangements that liberal societies enjoy today: the sacrifices that were made, the blood that was spilled, the lives that were lost, indeed, the world-altering convulsions that were endured. Many, if not most, of us inhabit a liberal landscape whose provenance is invisible. We exercise rights and liberties more or less the way we drink water: as things that simply are, rather than things that we have to fight for.

Sometimes it takes an outsider to bring things into focus and give us some perspective on ourselves, someone who can see things in us that we can't. The Canadian political theorist Bonnie Honig meditates on this theme in her fascinating book *Democracy and the Foreigner*. Immigrants, she points out, "enact" the rituals of citizenship in a way native-born Americans don't ever have to. First, in voyaging here—often at great peril—they've voted "with their feet" to live in America, whereas those born here are American by default, not choice. Those immigrants who decide to become citizens lift their hands and take the oath of citizenship—again, an act native-born Americans never undertake—and in so doing, proclaim or affirm an identity that is simply conferred to those born here. Foreigners thus play an indispensable function, Honig argues, in nourishing a democratic community and an active, as opposed to a passive, "performance" of citizenship. They can't take what we take for granted.

Some of that taking for granted seems to have passed recently. Since 9/11 outrage has erupted over the Patriot Act, the machinations of the Justice Department under John Ashcroft and Alberto Gonzalez, and the NSA's phone surveillance program. Thousands of Americans have mobilized in defense of civil liberties. The ACLU has robust new gusts of wind in its sail. Everywhere one turns there are books and articles being published on the subject. One can debate whether some of the rhetoric emanating from that mobilization overstates the actual threats Bush and Gonzalez (and Ashcroft before him) pose to civil liberties and the Constitution—I think some of it has been recklessly hyperbolic—but the fact is that however grave the threats are, they have occasioned a renewed dialogue about rights and liberties and a passionate affirmation of things that have, for many years, been more in the background than in the foreground of American political debate. In reminding liberals that we have to fight to defend civil liberties, the Age of Ashcroft has thus—unintentionally, of course—had a salutary effect on American political life.

Left-wing critiques of liberalism, which seemed in many ways to have lost their sting and appeal amid the revolutions of 1989, have been making something of a comeback in the Age of Bush. Whereas in the immediate aftermath of Communism's collapse, radicals like Peter Osborne were arguing that "the future of socialism seems now to hang in the balance of its reorientation towards the liberal tradition," liberalism now finds itself, if anything, on the defensive. Liberals are saddled with the burden of disentangling their project from neoliberalism, from the Iraq War, and from US imperialism. They are busy responding, in other words, to the radical critique of liberalism.

Marxists like Immanuel Wallerstein thus talk about liberalism's "essential links with racism and Eurocentrism"; radicals describe human rights as nothing more than "the rhetoric of empire" and characterize liberalism as a global "virus"; or, as a Marxist friend of mine put it recently, "liberalism is The National Security Strategy of the United States of America." Thanks in large part to Bush & Co. this kind of talk isn't easily dismissed. There is not only a receptive audience but a growing one for claims like Wallerstein's that we are witnessing "the collapse of liberalism and our definitive entry into the world 'after liberalism.'"

So as we teeter between boredom and suspicion, as we stammer between insouciance and jaundice about what I'll call Actually Existing Liberalism, it might be worth thinking about the upheaval in Iran today. By reasserting those values that we now take for granted, the Iranian struggle for liberalism can breathe new life into our own liberalism by reminding us, among other things, of how profoundly radical a force it is.

Habermas himself has made this point. He was invited to lecture at the University of Tehran in 2002. The event drew an enormous crowd—the auditorium was overwhelmed. His visit left Iranian intellectual circles abuzz. Study groups have since formed in Tehran to read his work. Reflecting on the experience, Habermas has spoken of his "encounters with intellectuals and citizens of an uninhibited, spontaneous and self-confident urban population" laboring under the weight of authoritarian rule. A young political scientist he met told Habermas that he "likes to return home [to Tehran] from Chicago, where he occasionally teaches, despite all the difficulties that await him," because in Iran, he told Habermas, "there is at least a political public realm with passionate debates."

And those passionate debates have high stakes. They carry deadly serious consequences for those engaged in them. First, because merely being a participant in political discourse in a closed society and having the "wrong" views can land you in jail or in a grave. And second, because the outcome of those debates could determine the future of your society. We're not talking about Oxford-style debating societies or mass-mediated spectacles like CNN's *Crossfire* (now fortunately in the grave itself). Iranians are trying to figure out what kind of society and political system they want. They're thinking through the essential questions of political life, and doing so at great personal risk—holding clandestine meetings in dormitories, reading Habermas and Berlin and Arendt and Kolakowski, pondering what role religion might play in a pluralistic, post-theocratic system, and brainstorming about how to get from here to there.

In a context like that, ideas take on vital, burning relevance: Popper's open society; Arendt's emphasis on the primacy of the political and her anatomy of totalitarianism; Berlin's distinction between positive and negative liberty; Habermas's notion of a legitimation crisis and his reconstruction of how the public sphere took shape in modern European coffeehouses; Kolakowski's insistence that there is

> one freedom on which all other liberties depend— and that is freedom of expression, freedom of speech, of print. If this is taken away, no other freedom can exist, or at least it would be soon suppressed.

These ideas take on an immediacy in Iran today that they simply don't have in the West. They are the intellectual raw materials of a revolution-in-the-making, a liberal revolution.

The great theorist of liberal revolution, the early twentieth-century Italian writer and agitator Piero Gobetti, believed that it was precisely the marginality of liberal movements—their being on the outside rather than the inside of political power—that underscored their radicalism. The Italian liberalism of Gobetti's age, of course, had to labor under the creeping weight of Mussolini's Fascism, which came to power while Gobetti was editing the journal *Liberal Revolution*, furiously writing essays, and being beaten and arrested (eventually dying from wounds inflicted in one attack by Fascists). This sense of battling uphill, of the precariousness of the liberal project, and the eventual experience of its being thwarted convinced Gobetti that liberalism was, at its best, a militant and revolutionary force. His writings are, in the words of the political theorist Nadia Urbinati, "witness to a liberalism conscious of its imminent and perhaps long-lasting twilight." But precisely for that reason they are a fog light in the historical sea of liberalism, illuminating the militant liberating power of the credo—a self-conception we liberals would do well to recover today.

I should be clear, however, that the parlance of "revolution" is far from the lips of Iranians today. Iranians are understandably turned off by revolution-speak, given the "revolutionary" regime they've been living under since 1979, but also—and this is criti-cal—because of the general failure of the revolution-ary Left in Iran. "The leftist, anti-imperialist ideas of the 1970s have given way to a more pragmatic discourse about economic and political dignity based on Western models of secular democracy," observes the Iranian journalist Afshin Molavi.

> Iranian youth largely dismiss the radical ideas of
> their parents' generation, full of half-baked leftism,
> Marxist economics, Third World anti-imperialism,
> Islamist radicalism and varying shades of utopian
> totalitarianism. "We just want to be normal," is
> typical of what hundreds of students have told me.
> "We're tired of radicalism."

Some sectors of the Iranian Left, moreover, forged outright alliances with Khomeini's forces—with disastrous results, both for themselves (upon fully consolidating power, the Islamic Republic decimated the Left, murdering thousands of its members and scattering the survivors into exile), but also, crucially, for its reputation and legacy among Iranians. As the dissident Iranian writer Faraj Sarkohi has written, "the left wing's co-operation with the despotic government and their rejection of democracy is firmly engraved on the memory of the Iranian people."

Their many differences aside, what united the Islamist and ultraleft wings of the Iranian Revolution was their virulent antipathy toward liberalism. "Death to America!" may have been the more famous slogan of 1979, but it is worth remembering that "Death to Liberalism!" was shouted along with it on the streets of Tehran. As many Iranian commentators have pointed out, the Iranian Left—not unlike its counterparts elsewhere in the world—lashed out at liberalism with a ferocious zeal, and this contributed to the Islamist ascendancy. This anti-liberalism was especially misplaced and ironic, given that the greatest anti-imperialist leader of 20th-century Iran, Mohammad Mosaddeq, was nothing if not a liberal democrat!

A painfully salient illustration of Western leftism's irrelevance to contemporary Iran is Antonio Negri's visit to the country in January of 2005 to deliver a series of lectures. Given the intellectually omnivorous climate in Iran today, it's no surprise that Negri was invited to lecture in Iran and that his talks were well attended. But most of those gathered found what the radical theorist had to say "oddly tangential to [Iran's] most pressing concerns," as Nina Power puts it. With the country's "widespread suspicion of classical Marxist or revolutionary solutions," she asks, "What exactly does Antonio Negri have to say to Iran?"

Most of the audience saw "little of relevance in his 'communicative, productive' model of mass political agency to what is, in many ways, a society constrained, at virtually all levels, by a ubiquitous, if internally riven, state." Negri's "concept of radicalism," writes Power, appeared to possess "no frontal relation to the constraints of the existing order" in Iran. If anything, Negri's message appealed more to the religious hard right and to Iran's conservatives, Power explains. "If there is to be a new Iranian revolution from below," she writes, "it is unlikely to take the form of a plebeian carnival or quasi-Biblical 'exodus'." (Ramin Jahanbegloo and I discuss this further in Chapter Four.)

Liberalism is not only the political tendency of choice in Iranian opposition circles today; it is the most radical force on the Iranian political landscape (and in the contemporary Islamic world more broadly, though I will limit my discussion to Iran). Contemporary Western radicalism simply doesn't speak to Iranian progressives. Why would it? The issues atop its agenda—anti-imperialism, anti-globalization, and (in a few remaining outposts) anti-capitalism—are not the central concerns of the Iranian opposition, which is fighting for democracy, pluralism, human rights, women's rights, freedom of expression, and freedom from theocracy. It's not that radical leftism is opposed to these things, but they don't form the core of the radical-leftist project. (The current radical bluster about human rights as an imperializing discourse notwithstanding, let it not be forgotten that socialists once made vital contributions to the development of human rights thinking, as Micheline Ishay discusses in her *History of Human Rights*.)

They do form the core of the liberal project, however, which is why Iranian progressives naturally gravitate to liberal thinkers. Ultimately, Kolakowski has poignantly remarked, "there are more important arguments for freedom and democratic values than the fact that Marx, if one looks closely, was not so hostile to those values as might at first sight appear."

Conversely, the Western Left has been largely silent—and flummoxed—about the liberal upheaval in Iran. One would have hoped to see the Iranian struggle figure prominently in the world of solidarity activism, or at least get some play in the left press—especially at the high tide of unrest, during the student-led demonstrations in the streets of Tehran in June 2003, which the regime crushed in a paroxysm of repression. Compared to the attention the western Left typically pays to student revolts in the Third World, the Iranian struggle has been virtually invisible on the radar screens of most leftists. In short, the tunnel-vision anti-imperialism of much of the Left (a current which has intensified considerably under Bush) leads down a dead-end of myopia and confusion vis-à-vis a case like Iran, in which the struggle is not being waged against the American Empire or its proxies. (See Chapter One for an elaboration of this argument.)

This silence has not gone unnoticed by Iranian dissidents. In hundreds of conversations I've had with Iranian intellectuals, journalists, and human rights activists in recent years, I invariably encounter exasperation: Why, they ask, is the American Left so seemingly indifferent to the struggle taking place in Iran? Why can't the Iranian movement get the attention of so-called progressives and solidarity activists here? Why is it mainly neoconservatives who express interest in the Iranian struggle? Afshin Molavi captures this all too well when he observes: "I know far too many Iranian leftists who have gone neo-con as a result of their feeling of abandonment by the American and European left. I wish they had not gone that route."

We need a radical liberalism to step up to the plate to fill this vacuum. Leftists have largely ceded on Iran because it doesn't conform to the all-consuming anti-imperialist paradigm; they're letting the imperialists, in other words, set the terms of the debate and thus do their thinking for them. Liberals have the right intellectual sympathies, with our insistence on the primacy of human rights, liberty, and democracy. But far too few liberals are willing to roll up their sleeves and engage in the kind of solidarity politics that the Left, to its credit, made a centerpiece of its activism, for example, in Central America and East Timor during the 1980s and '90s. That kind of activism necessarily involves a degree of militancy and intensity that liberalism isn't exactly known for. But it should be. We need to make our own liberalism radical again—to infuse it with a spirit of internationalism and solidarity.

Radical leftists have no monopoly on that spirit. In fact, they've dropped the ball on it repeatedly, in Bosnia and Kosovo, and now in Iran. When the Balkans were engulfed in a frenzy of murderous nationalism and death-squad terror in the 1990s, it was human rights groups, feminists, and liberal internationalists who took action while the radical Left either sat on the sidelines in silence or came to the defense of the "demonized" Milosevic. As mass graves were being filled and hundreds of thousands of people being dislocated, the likes of *Z Magazine* and *New Left Review* disgracefully turned their scorn not on the murderers but on the West; hell bent on squeezing the Balkan nightmare into preconceived Marxian categories, they claimed that the Western powers were intent on dismantling the last outpost of socialism in Europe—as if Milosevic ran anything other than the most vulgar form of gangster capitalism. Some even engaged in outright apologetics for the Milosevic regime and denial of atrocities.

Meanwhile, thousands of humanitarian workers, international lawyers, and human rights activists went to the Balkans and did something; the putatively "tepid" liberals at *The New York Review of Books* featured the Balkan cataclysm front and center in its pages, providing a vital chronicle of both reportage and analysis that stands in marked contrast to the muted, convoluted, and morally disfigured record of the radical intelligentsia. The Balkan episode should be remembered as one of liberal internationalism's finest moments.

Of course the geopolitical constellation that created that liberal internationalist moment and opened the intellectual space for the humanitarian interventionist paradigm to take shape seems to have been torn asunder by subsequent developments, rendered obsolete by the rampages of Bush, Cheney, and Rumsfeld. To be sure, the geopolitical equation and the terms of the debate have been dramatically refashioned. The principles of liberal internationalism may now be on the defensive, but they remain as vital as ever to struggles taking place around the world, and we liberal internationalists need to be avant la lettre in advancing its cause—from standing in solidarity with struggles like the one in Iran today to asserting the continued need for humanitarian intervention in places like Darfur.

In this period of widespread withdrawal from internationalist thinking—in which many self-styled leftists share the traditionally conservative suspicion that liberalism and democracy are somehow foreign to non-Western societies and represent an imperializing threat to their "traditions"—it's essential to underscore that Iran has had a robust and longstanding internal struggle for democracy. Indeed, write Ali Gheissari and Vali Nasr, Iran's is a "culturally indigenous and popular demand for democratization." "In Iran," they argue,

> the democracy debate is neither a Western import
> nor a concession to the West, nor is it a project of
> the state or the elite foisted on the masses. Here the
> debate is now a popular idea that has developed
> from within the society.

It's not simply as a matter of internationalist principle that we should reach out to liberals struggling around the world. We certainly should—but it's essential to emphasize that liberals around the world seek our support and recognition. Iranian liberals, for example, have said in no uncertain terms that they want our active support. When I interviewed the Iranian human rights lawyer and Nobel Peace laureate Shirin Ebadi in the spring of 2004, I asked her what she thinks of the view, widely held on the Left, that Iran's issues are internal and that western "outsiders" (writ large) should stay out of them. She firmly rejected this position and expressed a desire for "human rights defenders... university professors... international NGOs" to support the struggle for human rights in Iran. "All defenders of human rights," she said, "are members of a single family." "When we help one another we're stronger." It is important, she said, "to give aid to democratic institutions inside despotic countries."

Echoing this view, Akbar Ganji has said:

> We don't want anything from governments. We are looking to the NGOs. And we want people to know what the Iranian reality is, for people to know what's going on in Iran. The intellectuals, the media and NGOs in the world have to draw attention to the human rights abuses in Iran. We need moral support. I emphasize: we don't want intervention, we only want the moral support of the global community for our fight.

Both Ebadi and Ganji are keen to distinguish the kind of international solidarity they do want from the sort of "help" neoconservatives would like to visit upon Iran. Indeed, not only are they against military intervention in their country, preferring instead a nonviolent transformation from within; they don't even want assistance from the US government, which would only supply the regime with further ammunition against the Iranian opposition. Thus the Bush administration's announcement that it was earmarking $75 million to support Iran's democratic forces met with a resounding thud amongst those very forces, an unambiguous "thanks but no thanks."

Ebadi, Ganji and other Iranian activists thus reject both the radical Left's phlegmatic isolationism and the neoconservatives' dubious, itchy-trigger-finger imperialism. This gaping political void is screaming out for liberal internationalists to fill it. We can't leave our fellow liberals in places like Iran out to dry. Nor can we allow the impression that the neocons are the only ones in the West paying attention to them. Our solidarity is being sought out by our counterparts. Our internationalism demands that we listen and find ways to help them.

I'm calling for a liberal Third-Worldism, if you like, to take the place of the failed and moribund Third-Worldism of the New Left and its inheritors. Rather than cede the turf of the Third World to the revolutionary Left (as many liberals and social democrats have done since the 1960s), we should proactively claim that turf as our own, advancing liberalism as a superior framework to address the dilemmas facing the Third World today—parts of it in particular.

Fred Halliday identifies the defining properties of Actually Existing Third-Worldism, if you will, as follows:

a ritual incantantion of "no war" that avoids any
substantive engagement with problems of international peace and security, or reflection on how posi-
tively to help peoples in zones of conflict; a set of
vague, unthought out, uncosted and often dangerous utopian ideas about an alternative world; a
pleasing but vapid invocation of global human
values and internationalism that blithely ignores the
misuses to which that term was put in the 20th
century.

Now, to be fair, this doesn't apply to everyone
in the anti-globalization or global justice movement,
many of whom possess a more sophisticated understanding of the world and apply more intellectual
rigor than Halliday's polemic would suggest.
Nonetheless, there is a great deal of truth in this
portrait. Anyone even casually familiar with the political scene Halliday is describing knows that large
swaths of it are guilty as charged.

But pointing out the inadequacies of Actually
Existing Radicalism isn't enough. It's necessary, but
insufficient, to demonstrate the Third Worldist Left's
limitations and oversimplifications—to criticize and
emphatically reject its political monism, its tunnel-
vision obsession with US imperialism, and the myopic
picture of the world this creates. We have to go
beyond critique and propose alternative visions.
Where, for example, do we liberal internationalists
stand on the current architecture of global capitalism
(i.e. neoliberalism)? What is our position on things
like the Free Trade Area of the Americas (FTAA) and

on the Central American Free Trade Agreement (CAFTA)? What is our contribution to the debate about international economic institutions like the WTO, the IMF, and the World Bank and how they affect the Third World?

It's one thing to take the anti-globalization movement to task for not offering realistic solutions to these problems—but what solutions do we have to offer? How, moreover, do we respond to the radical argument that liberalism is complicit both in the neoliberal economic order and in the American imperial enterprise—that it functions as intellectual fuel for the machinery of Global Pax Americana? Again, we can—and should—spurn the vulgarity of such assertions. But what is the actual substance of our response to them? What exactly is our critique of neoliberalism and US imperialism? And how do we make sense of liberalism's complex historical entanglement with imperialism?

I don't propose any one set of answers to these questions. Given their tremendous complexity, there simply isn't the space to enter into, let alone come to any conclusions about them, in the scope of this essay. The point I want to make is that these are absolutely essential questions for liberals to confront and work through if we want to speak to the international arena and engage the Third World—which I believe we must. We're in our element on the Iranian and Bosnian fronts, in which the preeminent issues are, in the case of Iran, freedom of expression, human rights, democracy, pluralism, and secularism; and in the case of Bosnia, human rights, international law, and humanitarian intervention. That's the stuff of liberalism and internationalism—it's our home court.

But we have to be able to operate effectively away from our home court, too. Some struggles in the world today are tailor-made for a liberal internationalist analysis—but many are not. Where the core issues at stake involve the core principles of liberalism, our role is crystal clear. But where the core issues are poverty, development, trade policy, capital flows, financial markets, sweat shops, structural adjustment, landless workers, transnational corporations, ecological destruction, genetically engineered crops, and the like, we find ourselves on the home court of Marxists, anarchists, Third Worldists, and other radicals in the anti-globalization movement. It is generally they, and not we, who organize the forums and the demonstrations, who publish the magazines and the websites, who write the books and the working papers on these issues.

This needs to change. If we fail to engage the Third World ourselves, we will be seen precisely as "oddly tangential" to its most pressing concerns. We need to formulate liberal-internationalist and social-democratic perspectives on the most pressing concerns of the Global South—constructing alternatives to both Actually Existing Neoliberalism and its radical Third Worldist critics. We need to bring our collective intellectual energies and political sensibilities to bear on the global struggle for justice—on the economic and political fronts alike. To be sure, there are liberal internationalists and social democrats already doing vital work in this area. (Think of the work of Amartya

Sen and Martha Nussbaum around alternative models of development in places like India and Bangladesh.) But a much more aggressive and concerted effort is required.

The approach I'm advocating involves concrete, piecemeal, reformist organizing around, on the one hand, direct solidarity with workers in the Third World and, on the other, tinkering with the institutional architecture of the global economy (international trade negotiations, World Bank policies, UN Development Program projects, and the like)—insinuating ourselves pragmatically into those institutions and processes, bending the ears of green and labor-friendly bureaucrats to push for tougher environmental and labor agreements and the like.

These things are of course already happening, in the form of myriad NGOs, civil society organizations, and social movements around the globe. To be terribly provincial for a moment, there is an organization in my neighborhood of Chicago that I think worth mentioning. The US/Labor Education in the Americas Project (www.usleap.org) organizes highly specific campaigns in solidarity with workers in specific industries in Latin America—banana and coffee workers in Central America and Coca-Cola workers in Colombia, for example. They have no "revolutionary" pretensions; it's hands-on pragmatism, working within the existing framework of the global economy, but with the spirit (too lacking in liberalism, I think) of internationalism and solidarity—of rolling up one's sleeves and doing something concrete to support struggles abroad.

It's this spirit that distinguishes social-democratic internationalism or liberal Third Worldism from official liberal internationalism. The radical dimension of this vision comes down to the principle of solidarity: I'm talking about actively incorporating that principle into our approach to international politics, very much along the lines of the leftist Central America solidarity movement of the 1980s and early 1990s. Solidarity on the political front means supporting struggles for democracy and pluralism in places like Iran today and advocating humanitarian intervention in places like Darfur; on the economic front it means supporting the struggles of workers and others in the Third World/Global South.

Liberal internationalism tends to focus on the state, as well as global bodies, as the nerve center of political action. National and transnational measures are desperately needed, especially in cases of humanitarian intervention to stop genocide and crimes against humanity, but liberal internationalists tend to focus too much here. What's needed is engaging in direct solidarity with opposition movements and workers in the Third World, building active, on-the-ground relationships with dissidents and human rights activists in other countries—bringing them to North America on speaking tours; organizing (to the extent possible) delegations of western liberals to the Third World (and making individual trips); writing about their struggles in our magazines; spreading the word about what they're doing; getting the work of dissidents and liberal intellectuals in the Third World translated into English and disseminated; and the like.

That is, to make their struggle ours—and thereby to make liberalism itself more radical.

In doing so, we should draw strength both from our own accomplishments, like the Balkans, and also from the people with whom we stand in solidarity, as in Iran. There is much inspiration to be derived from the dissidents and bloggers and human rights activists struggling against authoritarianism and repression in Iran today. The militancy with which they assert the values of liberalism stand as a reminder of the vibrancy and enduring relevance of those values, not only in Iran but globally.

I'll close where I began, with Nafisi's *Reading Lolita*. Her book, she says, is about "how Tehran helped redefine Nabokov's novel, turning it into this *Lolita*, our *Lolita*." I would like to suggest that by looking closely at the struggle of Iranians today for human rights, an open society, freedom of expression, freedom to believe or not believe as one wishes, pluralism, democracy, the freedom to read whatever books one wants to read, without restriction—that if we take that upheaval seriously and see ourselves in it, the Iranians waging that struggle can help redefine liberalism, turning it into this liberalism, our liberalism.

CHAPTER THREE

The Necropolitical Imagination: Foucault's Iranian Odyssey Reconsidered

Between September 1978 and May 1979, Michel Foucault published a series of articles about the Iranian Revolution. Curiously, only three of them have ever been available in English—until now.

In their book *Foucault and the Iranian Revolution: Gender and the Seductions of Islamism* (2005), Janet Afary and Kevin Anderson have translated and assembled not only Foucault's articles on Iran but also interviews with Foucault on the subject (including one from an Iranian journal, translated from Persian), the critical responses of several of his contemporaries to Foucault's Iran writings, letters to the editor of one of the magazines for which he wrote the articles, an open letter Foucault wrote to Iran's revolutionary prime minister, and statements by Simone de Beauvoir and Iranian feminists on the revolution.

It wasn't until 1994, with the French publication of a four-volume collection of Foucault's occasional writings—a full fifteen years after the fact, and a decade after his death—that several of his Iran articles were rescued from the proverbial dustbin of history. But we Anglophones had to wait another decade—more than a quarter-century since their original appearance—for the documents to be bound together. The dossier, twenty-two items and one hundred pages in all, appears as the appendix to *Foucault and the Iranian Revolution*, while another 160 pages are devoted to a narrative and critical reconstruction of the entire affair, which, next to his work on prison reform, Afary and Anderson call "the most significant and passionate political commitment of [Foucault's] life."

The publication of this book is a major event in the world of Foucault scholarship, and it can be expected to generate a torrent of discussion, debate, reconsideration, and intellectual fireworks. Foucault's adventure in geopolitical journalism provoked considerable controversy at the time. In unearthing that controversy and forcing us to revisit it, Afary and Anderson's book is certain to evoke the same passions and push the same buttons that surfaced during the original dust-up, because the issues at the heart of the debate are still very much with us.

* * *

Foucault went to Iran in the fall of 1978 to write a series of articles about the growing unrest there for the Italian newspaper *Corriere della Sera*. He quickly developed an intense interest in what he saw unfolding around him, and was deeply impressed by what he called the emergence of a "political spirituality" in the Islamist wing of the movement to topple the shah.

The shah was forced from power, and although the anti-shah movement was a coalition of Islamists, liberal nationalists, revolutionary Marxists, and secular feminists (with some of these categories bleeding into one another, quite literally), Ayatollah Khomeini and his followers were able to consolidate their control of the new regime, not only squeezing most of the other factions out of power, but unleashing a bloodbath of repression against many of their members.

Foucault's chronicle of these events came in for tough criticism by Iranian and French feminists as well as some Marxists. At the time of the revolution, it became quickly apparent that the Islamists sought to turn back the clock "fourteen hundred years" on relations between the sexes, as one feminist group proclaimed. Yet Foucault, his critics argued, seemed barely to notice—let alone express horror at—the Islamists' virulent sexism. Reading his account of the uprising, you would scarcely know that forced veiling and beating of women by the Islamist wing of the movement had become rampant—the Islamist wing being the principal force that attracted Foucault's attention.

Foucault was, shall we say, less than engaging in response to his critics. He accused them of Eurocentrism, of antireligious chauvinism and of employing prosecutorial tactics against him. In one case he refused as a matter of principle to reply to a critique leveled at him. The situation under Khomeini's new Islamic "republic" deteriorated dramatically, with waves of repression against secularists, feminists, leftists, and homosexuals. Women were stabbed for refusing to wear the veil; leftists were rounded up, tortured, and made to disappear; and homosexuals were summarily executed.

With the exception of a single statement, Foucault's response was one of silence: "From June 1979 until his death in 1984," Afary and Anderson report, "Foucault never referred publicly to Iran." He did not attempt to come to terms with what had happened, nor did he provide any expression of support for the victims of the new regime's tyranny. How are we to make sense of this episode?

Philosophers aren't always known for having the sharpest political judgment. Perhaps because of the conceptual altitude from which they peer down at the events of their day, their political vision isn't always 20/20. Many students of philosophy are willing to forgive them for this and to chalk it up to naiveté about temporal affairs.

Afary and Anderson aren't quite so easy on Foucault. They fault him for displaying poor political judgment in his appraisal of Khomeini's movement. At the same time, however, they ask whether that judgment was connected to his larger intellectual project—or at least to certain aspects of it. They conclude that it was, and in important ways.

Foucault was hardly unique among Western intellectuals in throwing his support behind the movement to oust the shah—this was a cause célèbre on the Left. Where Foucault differed from many of his contemporaries was in hitching his wagon to the Islamist wing of the revolt (describing it as "beautiful") and in paying such scant attention to other elements of the anti-shah forces—including those of secular, liberal, feminist, and leftist persuasions. While French and American feminists like Simone de Beauvoir and Kate Millett stood in solidarity with their Iranian counterparts, Foucault viewed the modernist discourse of women's rights as foreign to the Iranian experience, as an orientalist superimposition on the religious masses.

Indeed, it was not despite the revolution's Islamist dimension that Foucault's intellectual-political juices got flowing, but because of it. He saw in the Iranian experience the promise of a whole different kind of rebellion—not just another national liberation struggle against colonialism, but something that went deeper: a revolt against modernity itself. Whereas third-world revolutions of the Marxist-Leninist variety were trapped, as Foucault saw it, in the language of the Enlightenment, the Iranians had chosen a different path—one that departed on a fundamental level from the logic of all modern revolutions and that promised not merely a new political order but, in his words, a whole different "regime of truth."

* * *

Why did Foucault interpret the events around him in the particular way he did? Why, in the case of Iran, did he suspend the deep-seated skepticism and anti-utopianism which so marked his overall approach to political questions? What exactly was it about the Iranian Revolution that animated Foucault and stirred his imagination, leading him to view the events of 1978-79 as world-historical in nature?

Afary and Anderson propose two keys to making sense of this. The first is political and intellectual; the second, personal and existential.

Foucault's intellectual project was, on one level, a critique of the Enlightenment and the modern Weltanschauung it generated. Where its proponents championed the Enlightenment as a "science of freedom," Foucault saw something quite different: the machinations of power and domination. In a series of landmark studies, he scrutinized modern institutions such as the prison, the clinic, and the asylum in relation to the rise of the so-called human sciences of psychiatry, criminology, medicine, sexology, and other fields. In stark contrast to the secular priesthood of experts who saw modernity as an explosion of progress and knowledge, Foucault viewed modernity as the construction of an elaborate panopticon, a gigantic system of surveillance and social engineering.

I'll never forget the initial impact of reading
Foucault as an undergraduate, the shock therapy of
being confronted with this picture of modernity. His
arresting, flabbergasting counternarrative about the
modern world has immeasurably altered the landscape
of contemporary scholarship—in the social sciences,
history, and the humanities. His depiction of power
and knowledge as inextricably interlaced, and the
image he conjured of modern society as a sadistic
prison house, are now burned into our collective
cultural consciousness. It is not an exaggeration to say
that we are, in one sense, all Foucauldians now.
But could it be, Afary and Anderson ask, that the
widely remarked upon one-sidedness of this astonish-
ing picture of modernity colored Foucault's understanding of the events he witnessed in Iran? Might his
fierce enmity toward modernity have led him to
embrace a revolt against modernity, and blinded him
to the dark side of that revolt?

The second, or existential, factor in the equation has to with the religious rituals Foucault
witnessed in Iran, and their impact on what we might
call his sexual imaginary. Foucault was deeply moved
by the penitence and martyrdom rituals he saw
performed in the streets of Tehran. During this
period, known as Muharram, Shia Muslims commem-
orate the murder of Hussein, the son of Muhammad's
cousin and son-in-law Ali; as a descendant of
Muhammad, Shiites believe, Hussein was the rightful
heir to the leadership of the Muslim caliphate but was
murdered by his opponents (the Umayyads) in a
bloodthirsty power grab. This dispute marks the fork

in the road between the Sunni and Shia branches of Islam, a feud that has important implications for Middle Eastern politics today.

Shiites mourn the massacre of Hussein and his followers through theatrical reenactment processions and self-flagellation rites; the mainly male participants in these passion plays chant eulogies, rhythmically beat their backs and chests with chains or sticks, use knives and swords to inflict wounds to their foreheads, and scorch their bodies. All the while, onlookers alternate between laughter and sobbing. "[Seemingly] oblivious to any sense of pain," some "cut their scalps in moments of frenzy," Afary and Anderson write, while others "smear dirt on their foreheads, indicating their eagerness to be buried for Hussein." Through the rites of Muharram, the authors observe, an "unacknowledged and unspoken, but clearly palpable, sexual energy is released on the streets." Noting "the whip and the little chains that the men twirl around to lash their shoulders," the French scholar of Iranian Shi'ism Yann Richard was struck by what he called "the sexual nature of this festival of death."

Death figures centrally here. Indeed, Foucault himself described Muharram as "a time when the crowds are ready to advance toward death in the intoxication of sacrifice." As the revolt against the shah grew, Muharram became increasingly charged with political symbolism, with the evil Umayyads representing the shah maneuvering to destroy Khomeini, who of course represented Hussein. Foucault was particularly moved by the "intoxication of sacrifice" he witnessed among Khomeini's followers, who were not merely willing to face their deaths for the cause, but seemed almost hell-bent on it—"more focused, perhaps, on martyrdom than on victory," Foucault observed. One is tempted to call it, to borrow Achille Mbembe's memorable term, "necropolitics." (Gholam Afkhami speaks of "thanatos on a national scale" in revolutionary Iran; Arshin Adib-Moghaddam describes the "'libidinous' idealism" of the process.)

My friend Max Cafard poignantly captures the psychodynamics at work here when he calls Mel Gibson's film about the final hours of the life of Jesus *The Passion of the Masochrist*. Whether in Christian or Islamic form, both are primal scenes of male suffering and physical agony; both are infused with the leitmotif of injustice and involve the internalization of guilt; both aestheticize violence and reach their climax in death; both contain more than a hint of sadomasochism and an undercurrent of homoeroticism.

In his 1993 biography *The Passion of Michel Foucault*, James Miller explored the interface between his subject's intellectual and personal preoccupations: Foucault's lifelong fascination with phenomena like pain, punishment, surveillance, and codes of sexual "normality" and "abnormality," on the one hand, and the penchant he displayed for sadomasochistic homoeroticism in his private life. Afary and Anderson attempt to connect the dots, as it were, between Miller's portrait and Foucault's writings on Iran. They link Foucault's intellectual intoxication with the Muharram rituals he witnessed to his fascination with what he called "limit experiences" that pushed the boundaries of life by flirting with death. In his book

The Art of Living: Socratic Reflections from Plato to Foucault, Alexander Nehamas celebrates Foucault's attraction to limit experiences as an expression of the eudaemonistic ethic of approaching one's life as a work of art. Let me be clear that I see no reason at all to criticize Foucault for this; I just don't think it's a very useful way to make sense of political life.

Adding a third ingredient to the mix, Afary and Anderson see all of this as intertwined with Foucault's quest, in the second and third volumes of his *History of Sexuality*, for an alternative sexual ethos to our modern, scientific, post-Freudian discourse of "liberation." In search of this alternative ethos, he turned to ancient Greece and early Christendom, which contained, in his view, more open approaches to sexuality, and particularly to homosexuality. In his book *One Hundred Years of Homosexuality: And Other Essays on Greek Love*, David Halperin wrote that Foucault reached into the past as an intervention into the present, in order "to discover a new way of seeing ourselves and, possibly, to create new ways of inhabiting our own skins."

In an intricate and gripping interpretation, Afary and Anderson read Foucault's articles on Iran in tandem with his *History of Sexuality*—which, they point out, he was writing during the period of his travels to Iran. He imagined in Iranian sexuality—particularly in the Muharram passion plays—precisely the kind of homoerotic openness that he venerated in the classical Mediterranean world. (In due course of time, it must be noted, theocratic Iran turned out to be considerably less open to homoeroticism—to put it

mildly—than Foucault imagined it might be.)
Nevertheless, all of these elements were at work, Afary
and Anderson venture, simultaneously: Foucault's
pursuit of an alternative sexual ethos in the past; his
personal proclivity for sadomasochistic homoeroticism
and attraction to death; the excitement of the arresting
spectacle of sexually charged religious rituals centered
on pain and martyrdom; and his hunger for a new
political spirituality that broke with both liberal-
democratic capitalism and revolutionary Marxism.

Afary and Anderson sum up what they take to
be the three points of convergence between Foucault's
postmodernism and Khomeini's anti- or premod-
ernism as follows:

> (1) an opposition to the imperialist and colonialist
> policies of the West; (2) a rejection of certain
> cultural and social aspects of modernity that had
> transformed gender roles and social hierarchies in
> both the East and the West; and (3) a fascination
> with the discourse of death as a path toward authen-
> ticity and salvation, a discourse that included rites of
> penitence and aimed at refashioning the self.

Afary and Anderson offer a feminist and leftist
critique of Foucault vis-à-vis Iran, taking him to task
for dismissing feminist warnings about the dangers the
Islamists posed to women and for downplaying the
authoritarianism of Khomeini's movement. They also
accuse Foucault of the very sin he accused some of his
critics of: orientalism. Foucault portrayed the Iranian
people as totally unified in their support for Khomeini
and his program of Islamic government. The clerics,

he wrote, embodied Iran's "collective will," a movement "without splits or internal conflicts." This, Afary
and Anderson argue, was empirically inaccurate—an
obfuscation of the huge divisions, for example,
between the many secular feminists in the anti-shah
movement and the Islamists, whose repressive
program was a threat to women's rights. It was a
projection, they contend, of Foucault's own sympathies and fantasies onto an Iranian context he knew
little about. The notion that Iranians think with one
mind was quintessential orientalism.

Just before his death, Foucault wrote a pregnant essay titled "What is Enlightenment?" to mark
the 200th anniversary of the publication of Immanuel
Kant's famous essay by the same title. In it, he seemed
to be shifting philosophical gears and reflecting on his
legacy. We should eschew, he admonished, "all
projects that claim to be global or radical." "In fact we
know from experience," he continued,

> that the claim to escape from the system of
> contemporary reality so as to produce the overall
> programs of another society, of another way of
> thinking, another culture, another vision of the
> world, has led only to the return of the most
> dangerous traditions.

Though Iran is nowhere mentioned in the
essay, Afary and Anderson suggest that the tragic
outcome of the revolution—to which Foucault lent his
enthusiastic support—formed the subtext to these
lines and weighed heavily on his intellectual
conscience. If they are right, Foucault can perhaps be

blamed for never making this reconsideration explicit. And yet one can appreciate his effort to come to grips, however quietly, with the experience.

Afary and Anderson are engaged in an admittedly speculative enterprise, and are thus wide open to criticism. Champions of Foucault disagree with the conclusions the authors reach. This is to be expected. Among the virtues of this book is that its publication of original source material in English will allow readers of Foucault to make up their own minds. The full text of everything Foucault ever published on Iran is here, in Foucault's own words, allowing "history" to judge and us to ruminate on yet another "philosophical-political profile," to borrow a Habermasianism.

In a sweet instance of the cunning of history, Foucault's ideas have, since his death, been deployed by some in Iran to unmask the clerical system and its operations of power—that is, as a tool of analysis against the very "revolutionary" forces about which Foucault had enthused in their inception. To his credit, I think this irony would have pleased Foucault a great deal had he lived to witness it. In fact I can just picture a mischievous grin on his face at the thought of it. Judging from much of the reaction to Afary and Anderson's book, however, it would seem that precious few of Foucault's disciples possess the master's appreciation for such irony, let alone his marvelous penchant for mischief.

CHAPTER FOUR

Ideas Whose Time Has Come: A Dialogue With Iranian Philosopher Ramin Jahanbegloo

Ramin Jahanbegloo, one of Iran's preeminent intellectual figures, was released in September 2006 from Tehran's notorious Evin prison, where he was held in solitary confinement for four months. No formal charges have ever been brought against him, but the Iranian regime has disseminated accusations that Jahanbegloo maintained "contacts with foreigners" and was plotting a "soft" or "Velvet" revolution in Iran.

Among the hundreds of scholars across the globe who signed an Open Letter to Iran's president demanding Jahanbegloo's release are Kwame Anthony Appiah, Zygmunt Bauman, Dipesh Chakrabarty, Noam Chomsky, J.M. Coetzee, Juan Cole, Shirin Ebadi, Umberto Eco, Jürgen Habermas, Leszek Kolakowski, Ernesto Laclau, Chantal Mouffe, Martha Nussbaum, Orhan Pamuk, Charles Taylor, Tzvetan Todorov, and Slavoj Žižek.

Head of the Department of Contemporary Studies at the Cultural Research Bureau in Tehran, Jahanbegloo's 20 plus books include, in English, Conversations with Isaiah Berlin *(1991), the edited collection* Iran—Between Tradition and Modernity *(2004), and* Talking India: Conversations with Ashis Nandy *(2006); in French, a study of Gandhi's political thought, an essay on the philosophy of nonviolence, a book of interviews with George Steiner and one with the Iranian philosopher Daryush Shayegan; and, in Persian, studies of Machiavelli, Kant, Hegel, Schopenhauer, Clausewitz, and Tagore, and works on tolerance and difference, democracy and modernity, and the dynamics of Iranian intellectual life.*

Ramin received his PhD in philosophy from the Sorbonne, was a fellow at the Center for Middle Eastern Studies at Harvard, taught political philosophy at the University of Toronto, and is the Rajni Kothari Professor of Democracy at the Centre for the Study of Developing Societies in Delhi. He is one of the founders of the journal Goft-o-gu (Dialogue) *in Tehran and worked on the magazine* Esprit *in Paris. In recent years Ramin has brought an endless stream of Indian, European and North American intellectuals to lecture in Iran—among them Fred Dallmayr, Timothy Garton Ash, Agnes Heller,*

Michael Ignatieff, Adam Michnik, Antonio Negri,
Richard Rorty, and the late Paul Ricoeur—effectively
acting as a kind of philosophical ambassador between Iran
and the outside world.

   The following interview was conducted via e-mail
in January and February of 2006.

Danny Postel: You've talked about a "renaissance of
liberalism" taking place in Iran. Can you discuss this
"renaissance"? Where does liberalism stand in Iranian
intellectual and political life today?

Ramin Jahanbegloo: Sartre starts his essay "The
Republic of Silence" in a very provocative manner,
saying, "We were never more free than under the
German occupation." By this Sartre understands that
each gesture had the weight of a commitment during
the Vichy period in France. I always repeat this phrase
in relation to Iran. It sounds very paradoxical, but "We
have never been more free than under the Islamic
Republic." By this I mean that the day Iran is democratic, Iranian intellectuals will put less effort into
struggling for the idea of democracy and for liberal
values. In Iran today, the rise of hedonist and
consumerist individualism, spurred by the pace of
urbanization and instrumental modernization after the
1979 Revolution, was not accompanied by a wave of
liberal measures. In the early days of the Revolution
liberals were attacked by Islamic as well as leftist
groups as dangerous enemies and betrayers of the
Revolution. The American hostage crisis sounded the
death knell for the project of liberalism in Iran.

But in recent years, with the empowerment of Iranian civil society and the rise of a new generation of post-revolutionary intellectuals, liberal ideas have found a new vibrant life among many intellectuals and students. The ideas and sensibilities that comprise contemporary Iranian liberalism were more or less formulated by intellectuals such as Muhammad Ali Furughi a century ago. Furughi's writings and translations of that period were mainly discussions of the basic norms of constitutionality and pillars of modern thought. For example, in a text called *Huquq-e Asasi Ya'ni Adab-e Mashrutiyat*, published in Tehran in 1907, he wrote:

> The government has two powers: first, the making of laws, and second, the execution of laws. If the powers of legislation and execution remain in the hands of a single person or a single group, the conduct of government will result in despotism.... Therefore, government is constitutional only when it has separated these two powers from each other and invested them in two separate groups.

The idea of separation of powers is one of the key concepts of Iranian liberalism today. For all those who support the idea of a referendum on and reform of the Iranian Constitution, the concept of "separation of powers," and not just "separation of factions" (as we have today in Iran), is essential.

But there is more to this, because Iranian liberalism is perceived by its supporters in Iran today as a more critical project than it was in Furughi's time. For the generation of intellectuals and politicians in the 1920s and 1930s like Furughi, Taghizadeh, Jamalzadeh and others, liberalism was a technique of progress, something to be activated as a universally executable program, irrespective of the local contours of culture. They regarded liberalism as a system of protocols that, when enacted by policy-makers, ensured the creation of institutions that enshrined the rule of law, and generated a rationally organized and governed public life. But the species of liberalism which has taken hold in Iran today, though it is complementary with the traditional wave of liberalism in Iran, is distinctive and decidedly original.

Thanks to the recent discovery and translations of the schools of liberal thought dominant in the Anglo-American world, as found in the works of Isaiah Berlin, John Rawls and Karl Popper, and an appreciation of older traditions of liberalism (Kantian, Millian or Lockean), a new trend of liberalism has taken shape among the younger generation of Iranian intellectuals.

Iranian liberals today do not deny that the liberties appropriate to a liberal society can be derived from a theory or stated in a system of principles, but their view of a liberal society is related to a view of humanity and truth as inherently unfinished, incomplete, and self-transforming. The principles of Iranian liberalism cannot be grounded in religious truth, because the very idea of free agency, as it is understood today by Iranian liberals, goes against any form of determinism (religious or historical).

In a country like Iran, where the logic of the theological-political is still absolute and where there is a single master-value, the principle goal of liberals is to fight for the idea of value-incommensurability that affirms a pluralism of ethical values and different modes of being. This is to say, the chief task of Iranian liberalism is to establish the proper balance between critical rationality and political decency. The lack of liberalism, symbolized by the rise of unreasonable and violent radicalism in the Iranian Revolution (both on the Left and the Right), committed a huge injury to our commonsense ways of political thought and political action, and led to deep confusion about questions of moral responsibility and collective human solidarity based on individual self-creation.

In more concrete terms, against the revolutionary model of citizenship a new model of citizenship is suggested by Iranian liberals who work as human rights activists, NGO organizers, intellectuals and students—a model defined in terms of the empowerment of Iranian civil society, the expansion of human solidarity, privately pursued projects of self-creation, moral education of the public and the development of the vocabulary of liberal democracy. The insistence of Iranian liberals on the concept of "civil society" as a space which stands in necessary opposition to the state is a check on the arbitrary and authoritarian tendencies in Iranian society. The creation of many voluntary associations, independent journals and reviews, and social and cultural NGOs as a genuinely participatory arena of civic engagement, deliberation, discussion and dialogue has played a crucial role in the promotion of civil society in Iran. As such Iranian civil society remains an important site of dissent and a battleground for Iranian liberals who try to bridge the gap between the formal structures of democratic governance and the cultural, social and economic conditions for the realization of democracy in Iran.

DP: The work of Jürgen Habermas is quite popular in Iran today. Can you talk about his visit to Tehran in 2002 and the effect it has had on the Iranian intellectual scene? Why do you think his ideas have caught on with Iranian students and intellectuals in the way they have?

RJ: Habermas's visit to Iran was a huge success. He was treated in Iran the way Bollywood actors are treated in India. Wherever he went or lectured, he was encircled by hundreds of young students and curious observers. This same phenomenon happened again when Richard Rorty visited Iran in 2004: around 1,500 souls came to his lecture on "Democracy and Non-Foundationalism" at the House of Artists in Tehran. Habermas's visit to Iran was an important event in the process of democratic thinking and dialogue among cultures. As Victor Hugo says in *Histoire d'un Crime*: "One can resist the invasion of an army, but one cannot resist the invasion of ideas whose time has come." The time of philosophical ideas have come in Iran. Today in Iran philosophy represents a window on Western culture, on an open society and on the idea of democracy. This is the reason why Habermas, Rorty, Ricoeur, Berlin, and many others are relevant in Iran. Most of the intellectuals in Iran today are struggling against different forms of fundamentalism, fanaticism and orthodoxy. Habermas is considered the inheritor of the Frankfurt

School's intellectual tradition that from the very beginning questioned all orthodoxies and authoritarianisms.

Actually, Habermas is the extension of a tradition represented by figures such as Adorno, Horkheimer, Marcuse, Fromm, and Benjamin who are all very well known in Iran. Today in Iran, those who are interested in Critical Theory focus a great deal on the works of these thinkers and there is a network of readers of the Frankfurt School who are also engaged with Habermas's work. Of course, Habermas's work is difficult to understand and it takes years of ongoing study to catch the nuances in both his theoretical and political writings. But the difficulty does not stop Iranian scholars and intellectuals from reading Habermas and translating his work.

I think there is also another reason why Habermas is so popular in Iran. It has mainly to do with the fact that with the failure of Marxist-Leninist movements in Iran and a new interest in Marx and Hegel, a younger generation of intellectuals and scholars are interested in rediscovering these thinkers from a new angle. The popularity of Habermas has also to do with the fact that he sees himself as a nexus in which Marxist thought is reformed, transformed, refined, improved, and brought forth to a new generation. Habermas's theory of communicative action derives largely from Marx but involves a systematic rethinking of Marx's ideas. Last, but not least, I think that Habermas' positive assessment of the Enlightenment and his insistence on its democratic potential finds its true place in the lively debate between the two concepts of tradition and modernity in contemporary Iran. What interests many Iranian intellectuals in Habermas' philosophy is his notion of "theoretical enlightenment" and the possibility of translating it into practical enlightenment. Habermas's advocacy of what he calls post-metaphysical thinking is of a great relevance to Iranian intellectuals today.

I think Habermas sheds new light on the problem of democratic agency through a new reading of Kant, Hegel, Marx, and Weber. I teach Hegel in Iran and I have made great use of Habermas' work in my Hegel scholarship. I think Habermas' reading of Hegel reinforces his approach to the philosophy of history, but it also consolidates his defense of the Enlightenment project as modernity's self-understanding. This goes hand in hand with Habermas' reading of Kant which is based on Kant's essential insight that there is no fundamental gulf between thought and reality, that thought and reality are intertwined in a primordial relation. Habermas' discourse theory appropriates the Hegelian theme of "recognition" and takes it a step further. Mutual recognition, understood as the mutual recognition of each other as free individuals, is a minimal condition in the Hegelian as well as in the Habermasian theme of recognition. Habermas transforms the original theme of the Hegelian master-slave dialectic into a communication-theoretical theme of recognition. I think that Habermas' Kantian view cannot be maintained without his explicit endorsement of Hegel's concept of "Sittlichkeit" and his dialectic of society and freedom, even though Habermas categorically rejects an objective teleology.

This brings me to Kant and Habermas. As you might know, Kant is a very popular philosopher in Iran and there were several celebrations in Tehran for the two-hundredth anniversary of his death in 2004. Well, once again as for Hegel, Habermas's recasting of the Kantian principle of autonomy and its political implications shows how public reason lies at the heart of democratizing processes and is decisive to the survival of non-authoritarian political, social, and economic institutions in our world. And you can see how Kant—and Habermas's reading of Kant—can be helpful in reformulating and re-elaborating a new democratic thinking in Iran. Habermas via Kant offers Iranian intellectuals and civil society activists a model of democratic agency and political thinking that avoids two unattractive alternatives: that of rooting politics in personal preferences for authoritarian personalities and that of eliminating the universality of ethics in the name of a revolutionary break.

DP: Hannah Arendt is also quite popular in Iran today. What can you tell us about this?

RJ: Arendt's work is well known in the Iranian intellectual sphere. Her ideas have been not only closely studied but acutely felt by many Iranian scholars. Three years ago I organized a series of ten nights on contemporary thought and the first lecture considered the life and work of Arendt. Arendt's work speaks in a vital way with new perspectives and new political and philosophical needs that have emerged among the younger generation of Iranian scholars and researchers. In a young and troubled Iran in search of a new intellectual culture, there is a serious desire to explore Arendt's oeuvre. If Arendt's contribution to political thinking finds an important place in Iranian civil society and among Iranian intellectuals, it is mainly because her thinking shows us how to recover the meaning of the public world. I believe that Arendt's popularity in Iran after the Revolution of 1979 is due to the fact that many among us saw a similarity between our experience of living with political violence and totalitarian ideologies (whether Islamist or Marxist-Leninist) and her own alienating political experience as a Jewish refugee who was excluded from participating in public life.

This is the main reason why the first translation of Arendt published in Iran was *The Origins of Totalitarianism.* Many Iranians had no idea in 1979 what a totalitarian state was, because most of us were in no way affected by the experience of Nazism or Communism. Actually for a long time the Iranian Left dismissed the claim that Communism in the Soviet Union and Eastern Europe were a form of totalitarianism. This reminds me of what Arendt formulates beautifully in her book. She says that

> While the totalitarian regimes are thus resolutely and cynically emptying the world of the only thing that makes sense, they impose upon it at the same time a kind of super sense which the ideologies actually always meant when they pretended to have found the key to history or the solution to the riddles of the universe.

I think Arendt's work on totalitarianism is key to showing us that evil is an important problem in everyday politics and that it has the possibility to emerge at any time and in any place. I believe that many have experienced in Iran what Arendt describes in *The Origins of Totalitarianism* as "the anti-political principle." It is the end of ethics in the political realm and the unlimited degradation of civic morality. In 1979 the abyss between men of civility and men of brutal deeds was filled in Iran with the ideologization of the public sphere. One saw the breakdown of the old system, followed by the failure of political liberalism and the formation of the ideologies of 1979. One can say that when common sense breaks down or becomes impossible, hopelessness and resignation set in; people lose the capacity for action and despair over their ability to influence things.

If the Iranian revolution of 1979 showed us that "anything is possible," Arendt on the contrary helped us to understand that thinking is an ongoing process which reclaims our capacity for action. I believe that Arendt's phenomenological reconstruction of the nature of political existence appealed to many of us as a way to uncover the originary character of political experience that has for the most part been forgotten in Iranian politics. Reading Arendt in Tehran reminds us continuously of the fact that freedom is "the ability to begin," and therefore civil society is a domain where people, in their collective plurality, remember who they are.

Another important fact that I think many of us have learned from reading Arendt is that pure action is free from everything because it is for the sake of the future. It is the eruption of freedom everywhere and in every situation without a political affiliation. Freedom is interruption and also beginning anew. Therefore, freedom is possible even in a world of secret police and of the rule of autocrats. Freedom is a universal human possibility. The space of public freedom is in essence finite, but the light of life that shines on the public realm can always begin something new. In a country like Iran, where you have a vibrant civil society, the most unlikely things happen on the margins of politics. What enables men and women, young and old, in Iranian civil society to bear life's burdens is the permanent challenge of keeping the free deed alive.

The point is that the taste for freedom and the experience of freedom can derive only from the diverse forms of participation in common concerns and community-engendering values spelled out in terms of a network of independent associations and institutions. Arendt discusses this in *On Revolution*, which was also very popular in Iran. If I am not mistaken in my reading of Arendt, I would say that her idea of "revolution" poses a big challenge to all those who continue to believe that revolution belongs to the realm of necessity in our world. The tragedy of modern revolutions, according to Arendt, is that what is actually revolutionary is the failed attempt to establish a political space of public freedom. This reminds me of what Malraux says in his novel *L'espoir*: "the revolution came to play the role which once was played by eternal life; it saves those who make it."

Well, I think that Arendt shows us very clearly that at the end this salvation in its purest form descends into restoration or tyranny, because all revolutions are simple hiatuses between liberation and the constitution of liberty.

DP: Why, in your view, are Iranian intellectuals and students generally not attracted to Marxist thinkers and ideas? Why do you think they tend not to be engaged by political currents like the anti-globalization movement or anti-imperialism?

RJ: It is not necessary to explore very far to find the reason for this lack of attraction to Marxism in Iran today. In Iran the number of "Marxists" was always a hundred times greater than the number of people who had actually read and studied Marx. This is the main reason why Iranian Marxism had so much trouble making sense of the Iranian Revolution. The Tudeh Party (Iranian Communist Party) and the leftist groups in Iran have no explanation today of their political and ideological struggles against liberal and democratic ideas in Iran. Most of these Marxist groups supported the anti-democratic measures taken against women and against Iranian liberals. Most of them, not to say all of them, supported the hostage-taking at the American embassy in Tehran. Some of them even backed the hardline clerics in the elections and contributed to the jacobinization and bolshevization of the Islamic Republic.

Now, I ask you the question: what do you think is left of the Left in Iran? Nothing! Some live in exile around the world. Some are doing business in Iran. Some have become collaborators. A few are good scholars who teach in American and Canadian universities. Many lost their lives and will never be back among us. I salute their courage, even if I think that they were totally wrong in what they did. Those Iranian Marxist-Leninists who continue to follow their traditional line of thinking have become more of an anthropological curiosity, because they continue to hide behind their mystifying appearances, whether political or other. These people continue to regard their point of view, after all their political and intellectual failures, as a privileged theory, because they believe that it represents the point of view of the proletariat and the proletariat is the class which realizes the passage to the true history of humanity.

There are two problems here: first, no vision of history, even if it represents the view of "the last class of history" that can bring an end to all action and discussion on and in history. Second, there is really no organized proletariat in Iran and the action and self-awareness of the working class in 1979*did not take shape in the direction of a socialist revolution; on the contrary, it was clearly in favor of the Islamic revolution. Actually, the equation was quite simple for the Iranian proletariat in 1979: "They [the Islamists] believed that there is no God but Allah, and Mohammad is his prophet; while the Communists believed that there is no God, and Karl Marx is his prophet."

The heyday of the Marxist intellectuals in Iran was over as soon as the Islamic nomenclature was firmly entrenched in power. Despite the great extent of its influence, Iranian Marxism did not succeed in the realm of great intellectual achievements.

Marxism's intellectual failure in Iran today can best be illustrated by the new attitude that one finds among the younger generation of Iranian intellectuals. The methodological position of the new generation of Iranian intellectuals is characterized by two main philosophical attitudes: the extension of anti-utopian thinking on the one hand, and the urge for a non-imitative dialogical exchange with the modern West on the other. To my mind, this problem of achieving modern conditions for rational criticism is in direct opposition with the tradition of Iranian Marxism. First, because new thinking in Iran rejects any pre-given consensus as a foundation, whether traditional authority or a modern ideology. Second, because it calls for an institutionalization of the public debate in the form of rational argumentation. Therefore, the real dividing line which runs between the younger generation of Iranian intellectuals and the previous ones represented especially by the Left is between the preachers of grand narratives and monistic utopias on the one hand and the admirers of dialogue and value pluralism on the other. The point is that the new Iranian intellectual is no longer entitled to play the role of a prophet or a hero. He/she is in the Iranian public space to demystify ideological fanaticisms and not to preach them. Today in a society like Iran where there is a systemic deliberation deficit, the sentimental leftist view of the intellectual as a vanguard(ian) of Marxist ideology is inadequate to the new Iranian reality.

In short, what all this means is that the new Iranian intellectual has finally returned to earth, to the here and now, after decades of ideological temptations looking for salvation in eschatological constructions. In other words, Marxism is no longer considered as a valid or sufficient theory for the explanation of social and political reality in Iran. In fact it is precisely the new social and cultural situation in Iran that has occasioned the younger generation to reconsider the method and the philosophical validity of Marxism in Iran. The re-examination of Marxism that is taking place does not occur in a void. Many have arrived at the point where they feel the need to choose between the ossified Marxism of the past and the project of radical change of Iranian society. We can call this process of re-examination a "pragmatic reaction" to the failure of what many considered to be "progressive" on the grounds that it would solve society's ills. In fact, not only were the ills not solved, but Iranian Marxism became an ill itself. I am reminded of what John Kenneth Galbraith once said about Milton Friedman: "Milton's misfortune is that his policies have been tried." Well, the misfortune of Iranian Marxism is that it has been tried. And it failed.

Concerning anti-globalization movements in Iran, as you know, like elsewhere, anti-capitalism has turned into anti-globalization among the left-wing groups. Most of the anti-globalization groups in Iran are those who mourn the downfall of the Soviet Union as a countervailing superpower, but you also find the critics of globalization among the Islamic groups close to the government. This has to do with the fact that the main source of anti-globalization sentiment is the resentment toward US military and economic hegemony. There is also a third group of young intellectuals who seem to be very much influenced by the works of Derrida, Foucault, Agamben, Badiou, and Žižek. The heavy influence of these authors on some Iranian students takes often nihilistic overtones that you can find expressed in articles in Iranian journals. On the other hand, you can find some democratic universalists and cosmopolitan intellectuals in Iran, like myself, who do believe that since globalization will not fully ensure the advancement of positive social agendas, we need to empower civil society in the domestic sphere, as it represents a countervailing power and prospects for better governance.

DP: You referred to Marxism's intellectual influence in Iran. What exactly has been the extent of that influence?

RJ: I think it is as necessary to understand why Marxism succeeded in influencing Iranian intellectual life as it is to understand why in the end it lost out in the 1979 revolution. There can be no doubt that Marxism and the Marxist movement registered spectacular successes in Iran despite not finally succeeding. There is also no doubt that Marxism has received a devastating political and ideological setback in Iran as elsewhere. Iran never had a working class comparable to the European proletariat of Marx's time. Marxism was propagated in Iran by the upper middle class and rich families, who were politically against

the Pahlavi regime and intellectually the most
prepared to embrace new ideas and to implement
them in the Iranian social sphere. From the 1930s
until the end of the 1960s Marxism was the doctrine
that provided the Iranian elite with an intellectual
grounding for a rupture with Islamic traditions.
Despite this vibrant interest in Marxist ideas—which
in the 1970s turned into a cult for guerilla warfare,
Latin American style—very few Iranian Marxists had
read Marx or were versed in the philosophical literature of western Marxism, such as the Frankfurt
School, Gramsci, Korsch, Lukacs, and so on. These
were too complicated and, in any event, little known.
If you looked at the books, pamphlets and political
tracts of the Iranian Marxist groups inside and outside
Iran, you would be horrified by the low level of philosophical knowledge and by the Stalinist tone and
content of the writings. Strangely enough, Marxism
was able to find a significant place in the hearts and
minds of many Iranian intellectuals for more than
four decades.

It's interesting to note that the influence of
Marxism and the activities of the Marxist political
groups in Iran fluctuated in direct proportion to
changes in the Iranian nationalist movement and the
influence of American diplomacy in the region. The
political and philosophical failures of the Iranian
nationalist movement headed by Mohammad
Mossadegh after the coup d'etat of 1953 helped put
wind in the sails of Iranian Marxism, which presented
itself as the vanguard philosophy of the revolution.
Also, events such as the Chinese Cultural Revolution,

the Cuban Revolution and the Vietnam War were influential factors in the spreading of Marxism among students and intellectuals in Iran. Lenin, Stalin and Mao were far more influential than Marx in shaping the consciousness and work of those in the Iranian Communist movement. Most of the members of the Iranian Communist Party considered (and some continue to this day to consider) Stalin as a great hero.

Most important of all was the lack of sufficient awareness among most Iranian Communists about the force of religion and the strong social networking of the Islamist groups in Iran. What the Iranian Communists lacked was an appreciation of Islam as an important social-historical factor in the formation and consolidation of the Iranian masses. Iranian Marxists, despite their ambition to be close to the masses, never spoke the language of common people; they were hopelessly out of tune with the traditions and idioms of the people. This got in the way of their progress as a revolutionary force, but not necessarily as intellectuals. They ended up after the 1979 revolution as unhappy intellectuals with no political party. This reminds me of Brecht's line: "Unhappy the nation that needs heroes." Maybe I could add in the context of what has been said: "Tragic the movement that cannot have the heroes it needs"!

DP: You mentioned the urge in Iran for what you call a "non-imitative dialogical exchange" with the modern West. This brought to mind a passage from an essay by our mutual friend Fred Dallmayr, in which he observes that there are often "more vibrant resonances" of European thought in a place like Iran than in Europe today. "This does not mean," he writes, in *Small Wonder*,

> that European perspectives are simply disseminated across the world without reciprocity or reciprocal learning. Nor does it mean that local origins are simply erased in favor of a bland universalism.... What it does mean is that landscapes and localities undergo symbolic metamorphoses, and that experiences once localized at a given place increasingly find echoes or resonance chambers among distant societies and peoples.

Is this the sort of thing you have in mind when you talk about a "non-imitative dialogical exchange"?

RJ: I am happy to see that you quote Fred Dallmayr in relation to my idea of "non-imitative dialogical exchange." Fred is a colleague and a friend with whom I have had many fruitful exchanges. We share a deep interest in Gandhi and India. I agree with Fred's view of a global or cosmopolitan discourse conducted along non-hegemonic lines. His idea of an alternative model of cosmopolitan interaction, inspired in part by Oakeshott's linkage of conversation with inter-human friendship has been very helpful for my own formulation of the idea of "democratic universalism." As you might know, in my debate with Richard Rorty during his visit to Iran, I suggested a distinction between two concepts of "universalism": a "soft" universalism and a "hard" universalism. "Soft" universalism provides us with a theoretical framework for various possible versions of moral life without being founded in a fixed idea of the self. In other words, "soft" universalism or what we can call "democratic universalism" provides a universalistic criterion by which we can scrutinize the principles of action that we might seek as basic to our lives, activities and institutions. Soft universalism does not force us to choose, but offers us reasons and arguments for adapting principles which we would adapt. In other words, soft universalism applies the universal right to reciprocity in a world of plural values in order to allow people with different values to accept one another. Unlike "soft" universalism, "hard" universalism is in search of uniformity and homogenization, because it does not accept the principle of cultural pluralism.

For many the paradox of the human rights corpus is that it seeks to foster diversity and difference, but does so only under the rubric of Western democracy. In other words, it says that diversity is good so long as it is exercised within the Western paradigm of liberalism. As a result, the center of the debate turns around the argument over whether or not Western democracy should be considered as a universal principle. Today in our world, Western democracy is challenged by religious fundamentalists and by nihilistic groups on the ground that it represents a form of political imperialism or hegemony. Well, I believe that even if democracy is not as easily spread or as deeply rooted as many American thinkers and politicians have assumed, there is no shadow of doubt that each democratic process is a potential ally in the struggle against the challenges of our century such as ethnic and religious conflicts, terrorism, poverty and environmental degradation. This is why I think that the idea of "democratic universalism" could be the best way of having a non-hegemonic implementation of human rights in countries where individual freedom is not the most fairly distributed thing. This goes hand in hand with the idea of a "non-imitative dialogical exchange" through which I suggest an intellectual discourse for redefining communities and individual-community relationships in a pluralistic way. I also refer here to Todorov's concept of "transculturation," which is very different from "acculturation." Transculturation is entering and living in another culture without necessarily appropriating its mode of being. Transculturation is the inclusion of new elements in an existing culture. It is the ability to grasp other traditions and to incorporate them into one's own system of thought.

Dealing with modernity in a dialogical way is having the right to speak back to it. And this response becomes in effect a part of the process of modernity itself. Therefore, a dialogical engagement is an open-ended process where the meaning is not located outside the subject but it is situated in the intersubjective relation of the two cultural subjects who are in dialogue together. In the model that I am outlining the subjects of the dialogue add to each other's identity in and through the dialogical exchange. A dialogical exchange among cultures is the only way in which our ignorance of other cultures and civilizations can be aired, our biases challenged, and our knowledge expanded. A dialogical exchange is the only way to negotiate different interpretations of the world without imposing one interpretation on others. So we are talking here about an exchange between two conscious partners based on a respectful confrontation of their experiences and the knowledge of the process.

So, there is no imitation in a dialogical communicative interaction between two cultural agents. I think countries like Iran, Turkey and Egypt deserve to be analyzed as societies which have imitated modernity for a long period of time instead of having a critical exchange with it. The result of this uncritical exchange with modernity has been the total subjection to different modes of instrumental rationality with no emphasis on the critical driving force of modernity which are, in Kantian terms, "escape from tutelage" and "public use of reason." Modernity is fundamentally about the reflexive making of history, and in this process the struggle for mutual recognition occupies the most important place. This struggle for mutual recognition arises from a dialogical exchange, because it is a mutual desire of respect. So it is accompanied with a demand that a person be culturally esteemed for his/her own sake. Of course, it is important to refer here once again to the concept of democratic universalism, which holds that there is an underlying human unity which entitles all individuals to basic rights regardless of their cultures. I will put forth the view that neither hard universalism nor cultural relativism is sufficient in coping with the increasing variety of human ontologies. That is to say, we have to look for a universalism which is founded on all human experiences of history rather than only on Western values. This is only possible through large-scale cultural encounters. Taking into consideration the ontological impact of these encounters, an outsider's judgment and discussion of local violations of human rights cannot be criticized as unwarranted ideological interference.

DP: You mentioned a number of contemporary European thinkers in whom there is interest among some young Iranians today: Derrida, Foucault, Agamben, Badiou, Žižek. Does Antonio Negri also belong in this group? I know that you brought him to lecture in Iran last year—which I found interesting, given your views on Marxism. Writing about Negri's reception in Iran, Nina Power, who was there, commented that his ideas were generally regarded as "oddly tangential to [Iran's] most pressing concerns." Negri's "concept of radicalism," she noted, appeared to possess "no frontal relation to the constraints of the existing order" in Iran. If anything, she observed, Negri's message appealed more to the religious hard right. "If there is to be a new Iranian revolution from below," she concluded, "it is unlikely to take the form of a plebeian carnival or quasi-Biblical 'exodus'." This sounds entirely consonant with your own thoughts on the failure of Marxism in Iran. Isn't it?

RJ: I know Negri from the time I was living in Paris. We are now close friends and I have been reading his writings with great interest, especially his work on Spinoza. I think there is nothing strange in appreciating Isaiah Berlin and Negri at the same time. This maybe has to do with the fact that I consider myself a politically moderate and nonviolent person, but a philosophically radical-minded person. I think philosophy is not only having a true sense of reality (as Hegel says: "Philosophy is its own time raised to the level of thought") but also knowing how to resist it. Philosophy is the daily practice of dissent at the level of thought. Being a true radical is having the courage to think and to judge independently.

As I told you before, what sounded fake to me in Iranian Marxism was that it was supposed to be a revolutionary philosophy and yet it produced ultra-conservative elements in Iranian society, who knew how to grow a Stalin moustache or put on a Che Guevara beret, but had retrograde ideas on social issues like women's rights or children's education. You can see the best example of this in the political attitude of the Marxist-Leninist groups in Iran regarding the first demonstration of women against the Islamic regime. Therefore, to make my point I would add that being a radical today has nothing to do with slogans, but has to do with the process of thinking differently. On this matter, Negri reminds me very much of Cornelius Castoriadis, whom I knew very well during my years in France. They both represent a generation of men of character and integrity who speak truth to power. I think despite the fact that many continue to consider Negri as somebody who, according to the former Italian President Francesco Cossiga, "poisoned the minds of an entire generation of Italy's youth," Negri is a radical mind that we need in the context of today's world. I think Negri and Hardt's *Empire* was wrongly characterized by many as a mystical and romantic invocation of a decentered postmodernist and post-imperialist world. Unfortunately, most people missed the important point of the book which is the discussion of the biopolitical context of empire. According to Negri and Hardt, the production of capital converges ever more with the production and reproduction of social life itself and it becomes ever more difficult to maintain distinctions among material labor and what they call immaterial labor. Those who are familiar with the works of the French philosopher Deleuze know that theoretically speaking Hardt and Negri situate themselves in the line of Deleuze and Guattari's *Thousand Plateaus*. One might not agree with the conclusions of Hardt and Negri's book, but one can say that *Empire* is a work of visionary intensity.

Maybe this is the main reason I invited Negri to Iran. His presence and his lectures had a great impact. For those of us who live and work in Iran, every visit of a prominent intellectual figure is a breath of fresh air which gives us the oxygen necessary to continue thinking differently. In Iran today, "intellectualism" is an accusation often concomitant with that of "being pro-Western," a deviation from the official line. Therefore, inviting intellectuals like Negri, Rorty, Habermas, Heller and Ricoeur is a way of crossing borderlines without leaving the country. It is a way of bringing into Iran the voices of other cultures so as to further cross-cultural dialogue.

DP: You mentioned your debate with Richard Rorty. What was the debate about?

RJ: The first time I met Richard Rorty was during my visit at Stanford. I was giving a lecture there and took the opportunity to meet with him. At the end of our meeting I asked him if he would be interested in visiting Iran and giving a few lectures. He kindly accepted and I organized his trip for June 2004. I thought it would be more interesting to have a debate with him rather than just having him lecture. So I asked Daryush Shayegan, an Iranian philosopher, and George McLean, Professor Emeritus at the Catholic University of America, who was invited by another Iranian institution, to join us on a panel. More than 1,500 people attended this event at the House of Artists in Tehran. Shayegan's presentation was mainly based on the idea that secular democracy now seems inevitable in the Islamic world, given the widespread rejection of revolutionary ideology and the diffusion of sentiment in favor of human rights. McLean's remarks were to do with democracy and inter-faith dialogue. Rorty's intervention was based on his idea of "post-democracy."

According to Rorty the golden age of bourgeois liberal democracy is now coming to an end. It lasted two hundred years, and it was good while it lasted, but we can no longer afford it. People are nowadays being easily persuaded to surrender their freedoms in the interests of "homeland security." As you know, Rorty dismisses the traditional aspirations of political philosophy. Unlike thinkers such as Locke,

Kant, and the early Rawls, who sought philosophical principles which could provide the theoretical groundwork for a liberal-democratic political order, Rorty insists that liberal democracy can get along without philosophical presuppositions and that democracies are now in a position to throw away the ladders used to construct them. In his speech Rorty came back to his idea that an attempt to ground democracy is futile because it is couched in an obsolete and naïve philosophical paradigm. In line with his anti-foundationalism, he argued that there is no way to reconcile universal and particular epistemological justifications. He directed our attention to the manner in which an anti-foundationalist position can yield ethical claims. Anticipating charges of cultural relativism, Rorty came back to his ideas on "human rights culture" and maintained that the claim that human rights are morally superior does not have to be backed by positing universal human attributes. I then presented my reply in an effort to elaborate the idea of a democratic universalism.

Considering Rorty's argument that the degree to which a "human rights culture" is likely to be persuasive depends directly on the degree of humility with which it is presented, I tried to show that Rorty's light regard for the political and lack of interest in the institutional conditions for realizing ethical ideals could present problems on the issue of human rights in the exchange between cultures. My point is that for many people in non-Western countries, the human rights corpus as a philosophy that seeks the diffusion of democracy and its primary urgency around the globe can, ironically, be seen as favorable to political and cultural homogenization and hostile to difference and diversity. As a result of this point of view, you can find many Iranian or Indian intellectuals who see universalism as the product of European history and challenge it as a form of political imperialism or hegemony.

As a non-Western intellectual who believes firmly in the ideas of democracy and human rights, I have been tempted through my readings of Rorty and because of my own experience as a civil society actor to seek a way out of this dilemma by finding a balance between the values of cultural rootedness and a sense of belonging, on the one hand, and the idea of shared, cross-cultural, universal values. Uneasy with the way Rorty seems to put discussion of the political on hold, I suggest in a very humble manner my distinction between two concepts of universalism. As I mentioned previously, "soft" universalism, unlike "hard" universalism, does not force others to choose, but offers them reasons and arguments for adapting principles which they might adapt. That is, "soft" universalism applies the universal right to reciprocity in a world of plural values in order to allow people with different values to accept one another.

I see "soft" universalism as the only hope for promoting democracy in non-democratic cultures. This relies on conscious cross-cultural learning and understanding. When cross-cultural learning can enable us to internalize democratic values, the possibility of moving in and out of any value system is preserved. In this situation, individual responsibility replaces particular values as the focus of concern. So we are talking here of universal values within a global democratic sphere. I think it would be extremely dangerous to have a dialogical exchange among cultures without a structure of shared universal values. In other words, I do not believe in international relations without an international ethics, especially in situations of power, violence and crisis. But going back to Rorty, I believe that his take on the desirability of human rights free of claims to their naturalness is an open-ended debate. But it certainly requires a long process of political and cultural argumentation and persuasion, one which many non-democratic societies, like ours, cannot afford for the time being.

DP: Is there interest in Noam Chomsky and Edward Said in Iran today? As someone who has interviewed Chomsky more than once, do you sense that his political outlook speaks to the contemporary Iranian situation? When you brought Fred Dallmayr to Tehran, he lectured on Said. What sort of response did he get from his Iranian interlocutors? Do the perspectives of Chomsky and Said—so paradigmatic in Western academia today—resonate in the Iranian context you have described?

RJ: Both Edward Said and Noam Chomsky are very well known in Iran and some of their books have been translated into Persian. I have met Chomsky four times and each time we had an interesting conversation on subjects related to the Middle East. Reading Chomsky and listening to him has always been very inspiring to me. As for Edward Said, I met him for the first time in Paris in 1996. I was introduced to him by Pierre Bourdieu and the Seuil publishing house. We had a long chat and I asked him if I could make a recording of my conversations with him. He kindly accepted and I later published my conversation with him in a book in Iran.

Through Said, I have met many other interesting people who were either his friends and colleagues at Columbia or were simply his readers and followers. I have invited some them to Iran. Among these, Ebrahim Moosa, Eduardo Mendieta, Ashis Nandy and Fred Dallmayr were invited in two different colloquia in 2002 and 2005, the latter a colloquium on Said organized at the Faculty of Social Sciences at Tehran University. Fred Dallmayr and the other participants presented papers on different aspects of Said's life and work and they were all well received by the Iranian students. My contribution to this seminar was on "Edward Said's Conception of the Public Intellectual as Outsider," which was published a year later in the *Radical Philosophy Review*.

The colloquium on Said was a premiere and it created a new wave of interest in him and his writings. Many of his later writings are now getting translated. It would not be an exaggeration to say that for Iranian intellectuals in particular and the Iranian learned public more broadly, Chomsky and Said are both considered as towering figures of contemporary intellectual life. This fame is not only due to their moral courage and intellectual audacity in facing the challenges of our world, but also because of their deep influence on

Middle East politics. Were Said still alive, he would be amused to know that he was being read, translated and remembered in a country like Iran. But one must not forget that Said believed in the universality of ideas even as he understood the importance of a location for their application. So he would have been against any misinterpretation or misuse of his ideas and writings by Islamic fundamentalists.

And this goes also for Chomsky. In one of my conversations with Chomsky, he makes clear his belief in the universality of human rights. Of course for Chomsky the Universal Declaration of Human Rights is not perfect and can be improved, but is a reasonably good expression of principles that people around the world accept. Chomsky stresses that the Universal Declaration of Human Rights was put together from many different cultures that were not Western imperialists. So there is a real universal aspect to this Declaration. In other words, according to Chomsky, the principles of human rights are reasonable principles because they express the consensus that most reasonable people would agree to. So, one can say that both Chomsky and Said defend a sort of non-hegemonic and democratic universalism. This is another reason for their status in Iran.

But I should add that Said and Chomsky are not only respected among Iranian intellectuals because of their radical and anti-conformist attitudes, but mainly because of their struggle against extremism and authoritarianism. For us, their struggle is a struggle against embedded prejudices of all kinds and against institutions (religious and non-religious) which aim to enslave people. I think that Said and Chomsky are also important to us because their intellectual task has been a perpetual struggle against the negative role played by the media in sidelining and covering, if not altogether eliminating "undesirable" news. I think Said and Chomsky represent good examples of intellectual integrity and responsibility. Their continuous struggle and hard work is a testimony to the role of the intellectual in today's world and the intellectual's position as an "outsider" but also as a critical traveler of cultures and traditions in the age of the global village. Today the struggle of intellectuals in Iran is not only a quest for pluralism, but also a vital quest for ethical truth and human dignity, situating the intellectual endeavor in its responsible context. To have a free spirit and to be an unrelenting force for integrity is not a simple task for those who are confronted with lies on a daily basis. Few figures have been able to bring together the radical denunciation of cultural and political hegemony with such a deeply felt commitment to democratic universalism as Said and Chomsky. Today reading Said and Chomsky in Tehran is like living life at the edge. It is risky but full of excitement and exhilaration. Not only because they challenge us continuously through their writings but because they ingrain in us the value of intellectual integrity, which is of the essence in the most challenging of situations.

DP: You have expressed a deep respect that you and other Iranians feel for Chomsky and Said in broad terms, as intellectuals. But I want to focus for a moment on the political content of their ideas. Let me rephrase my question this way. You've painted a picture of a liberal renaissance in Iran today, of an intellectual landscape in which liberal thinkers and ideas, generally speaking, hold more sway than do radical/Marxist ones; a milieu in which the language of democracy, rights, and pluralism has a deeper reso-nance than does the language of anti-imperialism, anti-globalization, and anti-capitalism. Although you're certainly right to emphasize the universalism and humanism of both Chomsky and Said, there's no avoiding the fact that the central issue around which their political writings revolve is that of imperialism. Anti-imperialism is not the animating spirit or the central issue for Iranian liberals, whereas anti-imperi-alist and Third Worldist motifs formed the core of the Iranian Marxist paradigm, which—as you pointed out earlier—was a failed project that the younger genera-tion of Iranian intellectuals largely rejects. Given this, it would seem to me that Chomsky and Said, as para-digmatic figures of anti-imperialist thought, would have less direct political relevance in the context of the Iranian liberalism. Is there not something of a tension or disjuncture here, between the liberal-democratic-pluralist project and the radical anti-imperialist one?

RJ: One can be a liberal and be anti-imperialist. As you know, there is a tradition of anti-imperialist liber-als in the West. Classical liberalism was stridently anti-imperialist. English liberals denounced British empire-building. By reading J.A. Hobson's book *Imperialism: A Study* (first published in 1902) you could find a Fabian line of criticism of the British Empire. The book is partly a response to the Boer War and it was very influential on Lenin, who regurgitated Hobson's ideas with a Marxian twist. Hobson says very correctly that "Imperialism is a depraved choice of national life, imposed by self-seeking interests." The classical liberal sociologist William Graham Sumner was also a strong anti-imperialist who explained twentieth-century US foreign policy quite clearly when he wrote:

> We were told that we needed Hawaii in order to secure California. What shall we now take in order to secure the Philippines? No wonder that some expansionists do not want to "scuttle out of China." We shall need to take China, Japan, and the East Indies, according to the doctrine, in order to "secure" what we have. Of course this means that, on the doctrine, we must take the whole earth in order to be safe on any part of it, and the fallacy stands exposed. If, then, safety and prosperity do not lie in this direction, the place to look for them is in the other direction: in domestic development, peace, industry, free trade with everybody, low taxes, industrial power.

So one can talk about an anti-imperialist liberal tradition in the West, even if it was weak in its institutional continuity in a country like the United States. If we turn to contemporary Iranian history, we see clearly someone like Mossadeq, who was both a liberal and an icon of anti-imperialism in the developing world. By blocking liberal, secular nationalism in

1953, the Americans unwittingly played an important role in ensuring the rise of Islamic fundamentalism in that country a quarter of a century later.

Now to get back to Said and Chomsky and how I think they can be read and practiced by Iranian liberals, let me quote a line from the American judge Learned Hand that I have always liked and cited: "The spirit of liberty is the spirit which is not too sure that it is right." I think this is the best way of being a liberal today. There is a difference between this mode of thinking and neo-liberal thought. To say that reality and truth are the sole properties of Western liberalism is ideological demagoguery. To me being a liberal means having more of a moral predicament than a political mandate. So one cannot be a critical liberal and put imperialism before pluralism. And when I say pluralism, I mean a non-dominative exchange. This means that by positing a universality of human experience, we should stand outside the constraints of political and financial dependencies. So what Said elaborates as "outsiderhood" in his thinking is an important cornerstone not only to a cross-cultural dialogue, but also to the situation of critical marginality that an intellectual should have. I agree fully with Said that being an "outsider" does not mean cultivating one's garden, but rather experiencing life as an "unstable cluster of flowing currents."

So I situate myself on the side of people like Said and Chomsky, as someone who stands at a distance from a tradition, in order to be able to develop his critical capacities in regard to that tradition. This is how one can be a liberal pluralist and a secular humanist and be at the same time an anti-impe-rialist. It has to do not only with creating an alternative narrative but also resisting the hegemonic narratives that block us from forming and consolidating this counter-narrative. I think Empire is not merely a polit-ical relationship of power and domination, but revolves around the power to control the other's state of mind. Therefore, the job of a critical intellectual is neither to accept the dominion of another culture, nor to get swallowed by a nativist politics of identity which ends up with a culturally relativist or fundamentalist atti-tude. This also means that fighting for democracy and values such as pluralism in a country like Iran or Iraq does not necessarily mean accepting the American way of life. This is a fact that Americans have become aware of very recently. The truth is that what America has to say about other people and other cultures is now challenged by those people themselves. I thing the phenomenon of "American exceptionalism" is in itself a major obstacle to a just and equal cross-cultural dialogical exchange. Arabs, Turks, Iranians, Indians and many others are no longer living on the "periphery" of history, because there is no longer any one center anywhere; we have all become centers.

DP: Although you, Ramin, value and derive insight from the work of both liberal-pluralist thinkers like Berlin and radical anti-imperialist thinkers like Said and Chomsky, are Said and Chomsky as popular among Iranians today—young Iranians in particular—as are Berlin and Habermas?

RJ: You are absolutely right about Berlin, Popper, and Habermas being more popular in Iran than Said and Chomsky. This is mainly due to the fact that philosophy has become fashionable among Iranian students. It is surprising to see the level of interest of Iranian youngsters in philosophy. Even in some recent Iranian films you can see the main characters reading philosophy books written by contemporary Iranian or western philosophers. I have personally organized seminars on Hegel and Kant in Yazd, Isfahan, and many other urban areas of Iran. I am always amazed to see the level of interest of Iranian youth in philosophy. I think this is because philosophy is experienced as a mode of resistance against political ideologies and religious dogmatism. Reading philosophical texts in Iran today is like reading Patocka and Husserl in Prague in the late 1970s. So no wonder Berlin, Habermas, Rorty, Foucualt, Derrida, Ricoeur, and others are far more popular than Chomsky. What interests Iranian youth in Chomsky and Said is their critique of American foreign policy in the Middle East. But as I mentioned earlier, Iranian students have other ideas in mind. Their discussions turn around concepts like democracy, pluralism, civil society, tradition and modernity, religious tolerance, and the like.

As for the intellectuals, they are not a monolithic group. In regard to philosophy and philosophical readings, one can identify three tendencies in their discourses. The first tendency is secular. Secular intellectuals do not attempt to promulgate any ideologies or to struggle for the establishment of an Islamic democracy in Iran (as do the religious reformist intel-

lectuals) and yet they undermine the main philosophical and intellectual concepts of the established order.
Among them you have post-revolutionary intellectuals, such as Javad Tabatabai, Babak Ahmadi, Hamid
Azodanloo, Moosa Ghaninejad, and Nasser Fakouhi,
who are in their late forties and fifties, and who can
be referred to as the "dialogical intellectuals" (in
contrast with the revolutionary intellectuals of the
1970s and early 1980s). In other words, for the secular intellectuals, the concept and the practice of
dialogue provide an ontological umbrella for all political and cultural meanings and understandings. The
very objective of this "culture of dialogue" is to move
beyond seeing the other as an "enemy" who must be
terminated either as an individual or as a social class,
and to promote a full acknowledgement of the other
as a subject. In this case different intellectual attitudes
are asked to co-exist side by side to find an intersubjective basis for their encounter with modernity and
democracy. This move away from master ideologies is
echoed by a distrust of all metaphysically valorized
forms of monist thinking. Unlike the previous gener-
ations of leftist and religious intellectuals, what the
critical engagement with modernity has taught secular
intellectuals in Iran is to be at odds with both fundamentalist politics and with utopian rationalities. The
secular intellectuals are mainly influenced by Kant,
Hegel, Nietzsche, Berlin, Hayek, Popper, Foucault,
and Ricoeur.

The second and third tendencies are both
based on religious thought, but are divided by political and epistemological differences. On the one hand,

we find the reformists and on the other hand we find the neo-conservatives. The reformist group is represented by figures such as Abdolkarim Soroosh, Mohsen Kadivar, Alavi-Tabar, Hassan Yousefi Eshkevari, Mojtahed Shabestari, and many others. The unifying trait of these intellectuals is their attempt to reconcile Islamic thought with democracy, civil society and religious pluralism and their opposition to the absolute supremacy of the Supreme Guide (velayat-e faqih). The rise of religious intellectuals can be followed through the writings of Soroosh. Soroosh's main idea is that there are perennial unchanging religious truths, but our understanding of them remains contingent on our knowledge in the fields of science and philosophy. Unlike Ali Shariati, who turned to Marxism to bring a historicist perspective to Shiite thought, Soroosh debates the relation between democracy and religion and discusses the possibility of what he calls "Islamic democracy." What Soroosh, who's now living in England, has been trying to do during the past decade is convince his fellow citizens that it is possible to be Muslim and to believe in democracy. Soroosh stresses that there are two views of religion, a maximalist and a minimalist one. In the maximalist view, according to him, everything has to be derived from religion, and most of the current problems in Islam come from this view. But the minimalist view implies that some values cannot be derived from religion, like respect for human rights. For Soroosh the maximalist view of religion has to be replaced by a minimalist view, or else the balance between Islam and democracy is not possible.

Thus for Soroosh a democratic Islamic society would not need any Islamic norms from above.

Mojtahed Shabestari is among the rare religious intellectuals in Iran who has challenged the monistic view of Islam. According to Shabestari, the official Islamic discourse in Iran has created a double crisis. The first crisis is due to the belief that Islam encompasses a political and economic system offering an answer relevant to all historical periods; the second crisis is entailed by the conviction that the government has to apply Islamic law (shariah) as such. These two ideas have emerged, according to Shabestari, in relation to the Islamic revolution and the events that followed it. But the fact is, according to Shabestari, that Islam does not have all the answers to social, economic and political life at all points in history. Also, there is no single hermeneutics of Islam as such. Therefore, the relation between religion and ideology is simply unacceptable and leads to the desacralization of religion. Strangely enough, the reformist intellectuals have also been influenced by thinkers such as Kant and Popper (but less by thinkers such as Foucault or Derrida).

Unlike the reformist intellectuals, the neo-conservative intellectuals in Iran are in favor of the absolute supremacy of the Supreme Guide and against concepts such as democracy, civil society and pluralism. This movement includes figures such as Reza Davari Ardakani, Qolam-Ali Haddad Adel, Gholam Reza Awani, and Mehdi Golshani. The famous personality among these is Reza Davari-Ardakani, who an anti-Western and anti-modern philosopher deeply engaged with the work of Martin Heidegger. Davari-Ardakani, unlike Soroosh, takes some of the features of Heidegger's thought, mainly his critique of modernity, and frames it in Islamic terms. He rejects the Western model of democracy, which is based on the separation of politics and religion. President of the Iranian Academy of Science, Davari-Ardakani could be considered the philosophical spokesman of the Islamic regime. There is a temptation among the conservative intellectuals to find an affinity between Heideggerianism and Islamic thought. We thus find no readings of Said, Popper, or Berlin among this last group. Even those like Haddad Adel (the president of the Iranian parliament) who are interested in Kant make no hay of his moral and political writings.

So it is safer to say that there are varied intellectual currents in Iran and there are multiple readings of the Western canon. This actually creates an opportunity for pluralism in the Iranian intellectual arena, which has been absent for many decades because of the cultural agendas pursued both by the Pahlavi regime and the Islamic Republic. But it had also to do with the ideological predominance of the Marxist and Islamic ideas among Iranian intellectuals in the 1960s, 1970s, and 1980s. This ideological predominance has posed both philosophical and practical problems today in Iran.

DP: What, if anything, can liberals outside of Iran do to support Iranian liberals? There are many who argue that Iran's issues are internal and that western "outsiders" should stay out of them (a view shared by both Islamists and many Marxists, it's worth noting). When I interviewed Shirin Ebadi, she firmly rejected this position and expressed a desire for "human rights defenders... university professors... international NGOs" to support the struggle for human rights in Iran. "All defenders of human rights," she said, "are members of a single family." "When we help one another we're stronger." As an internationalist and a universalist, what are your thoughts on this question?

RJ: I fully agree with Shirin Ebadi on this issue. Of course, as you know this intellectual attitude is not new. It goes back to the eighteenth century. I always take pleasure in reading and teaching Thomas Paine, the great British-born liberal who writes in his pamphlet *Common Sense*:

> Every spot of the old world is overrun with oppression. Freedom hath been hunted round the globe. Asia, and Africa, have long expelled her. Europe regards her like a stranger, and England hath given her warning to depart. O! receive the fugitive, and prepare in time an asylum for mind.

Well, one can say that the violation of freedom and democracy and disrespect of individual liberties in different parts of the world continue as in Paine's time. Since the idea of human rights transcends local legislation and the citizenship of the individual, the support for human rights can come from anyone— whether or not she is a citizen of the same country as the individual whose rights are threatened. A foreigner does not need the permission of a repressive government to try to help a person whose liberties are being violated. Because insofar as human rights are seen as rights that any person possesses as a human being (and not as a citizen of any particular country), the reach of the corresponding duties can also include any human being, irrespective of his/her particular citizenship.

So I am a human rights universalist, but I do not think that one can enforce human rights and liberal values through violence or military force. I am, however, for humanitarian intervention, as it is practiced by human rights activists and NGOs around the world. The universality of human rights should not be turned into a double standard. Human rights provide us with a standard of conduct which no one can now ignore. Human rights are primary core values of human civilization. They are far from being perfect, but they are the cornerstones of our daily struggle for human dignity around the world. Protecting human dignity is not only about protecting oneself from violence but also defending the other.

So there should be firm grounds for moral objection when people's rights are violated in another society. For me one of the essential problems today is to promote cross-cultural harmony. For relativists, as Clifford Geertz has argued, "humans are shaped exclusively by their culture and therefore there exist no unifying cross-cultural human characteristics." I think this is to say that there are no ultimate standards of right and wrong by which to judge cultures. If this becomes true, we all turn into passive spectators of naked violence happening in front of our eyes. Of course I don't think religion can be used to judge our actions as right or wrong, because religion provides us with a fixed moral philosophy. But there are ethical standards that transcend political actions in international relations. I think there should be an equal submission of all to a minimal set of universal ethical rules. This is how the struggle for the liberal values of pluralism and negative liberty can join the universal values of critical cosmopolitanism. It is a route that leads from Kant's idea of a universal history from a cosmopolitan point of view to Fred Dallmayr's vision of "our world." Values and norms do not remain unaffected by what I regard as cross-cultural exchange and learning. There is no one way of life suitable to all individuals around the globe, and reasonable people therefore can and must have reasonable discussions and arguments about human values as they are practiced in different cultures. This means that against moral relativism and hegemonic universalism from above we can build a cosmopolitan democracy from bellow. In other words, we have to take up the challenge of defending the classical values of liberalism by promoting the spirit of cosmopolitanism and tolerance for diversity. After all, cosmopolitanism in essence means opening to others, accepting differences and living with plurality. But it also means going beyond one's own national prides and prejudices and giving allegiance to humanity.

I'm not talking about a universal culture that situates itself against particular experiences of local cultures. But it is a middle way between neo-liberal universalist interventionism and particularist identity

positions. I think liberals around the world can join
Kant and say with him that the global public sphere is
the place in which the private interests of members of
global civil society can be reconciled with the universal
moral obligations of membership in a "kingdom of
ends," a kingdom in which individuals and relationships are treated as ends in themselves, and not simply
means to other ends. That is to say, no one can pretend
today in America, Europe or the Middle East to
believe in liberal values and not have a sense of solidarity with individuals who are fighting for their dignity.
We need to think hard about the meaning of solidarity.
Solidarity is not about supporting those who share
your precise view of politics. It's about supporting
those who struggle against injustice and violence and
who fight for democracy. The real hope for democrats
in Iran is that this sense of the word "solidarity" be
understood by humanists, liberals and cosmopolitans
around the world.

DP: You have made a most eloquent intellectual case
for a cosmopolitan perspective. But let me ask you on
a very practical level: what can we liberal internationalists and democratic pluralists living outside of Iran
do, concretely speaking, for our Iranian counterparts?
How can we be of assistance to you in your struggle?

RJ: I think the first thing to do is to recognize the
fact that there are democratic pluralists in Iran fighting for democratic values and civil liberties. Their
struggle for the empowerment of Iranian civil society
goes beyond a simple act of contestation. The process

of democratization in Iran is a day-to-day challenge which is not only political, but also social and cultural.

Democracy is not a place where you sit and relax for the rest of your life. It is about responsible civic participation and intellectual integrity. So without this sense of responsibility I don't see how we could manage to have a strong civil society wherein people find their confidence in speaking and acting.

Pascal used to say that "We are usually convinced more easily by reasons we have found ourselves than by those which have occurred to others." This is very true of our situation in Iran. The actors in Iranian civil society need to find their own logics and practices of togetherness rather than those imposed on them. But this cannot be done without intellectual maturity. Maturity is the condition of possibility for pluralism in Iranian civil society. I am referring here to the Kantian idea of moral responsibility based on intellectual maturity. As you know, Kant defines immaturity as one's inability to use one's own understanding without the guidance of another. In other words, the public use of reason is the true condition of democratic life. Therefore, our aim in Iranian civil society is to create a horizontal line of critical reasoning in the public sphere.

I sincerely believe that finding a place for philosophical debates in the Iranian public sphere today is the highest level of political maturity. This is how our counterparts in the West or the East could be helpful. I have been trying to invite writers, philosophers and scholars from different parts of the world here in order to help them understand Iran but also to open up intellectual discussions with them on subjects that are of great interest to us. Iranian students are eager to know more about Western cultures and are curious to discuss their views on religion, democracy, philosophy and culture with western intellectuals. What they ask for is not sympathy but empathy. They have an eagerness to learn from others and through this learning to become more mature. What remains most fundamentally true is that "empathy" as opposed to "apathy" is the most desirable, even the definitive, philosophical state in our struggle for political maturity. A civil society like ours which is experiencing an alternative form of togetherness on a daily basis requires empathy and solidarity. Empathy is for us the condition of belonging to a global public sphere.

Consequently, we cannot undergo a process of redefinition of our political self without having created this situation of empathy with others. It seems clear that in our philosophical quest for maturity we need to address the question of empathy in the sense of what Husserl called "experiencing someone else." This is where your notion of "solidarity" finds its true meaning. If we understand by "solidarity" getting involved with another's community to create change, then the best form of solidarity with Iranian liberals is to engage in a comprehensive and empathetic dialogue with them. Liberal ideas are new to a country like Iran. They are only one hundred years old. To internalize them, Iranian civil society needs to know them better. This cannot be done by violence or by exporting ideas. We need to have more debates among us. Internationalism, liberalism, and democracy are powerful concepts and have indeed begun to dominate all of the debates within Iranian civil society. But we need to examine them together critically. This is where the concept of maturity links up with that of solidarity. Solidarity does not mean charity, it does not mean intervention and it cannot be reduced to altruism. Rather it is something which grows out of an understanding of common responsibility. It is in our common responsibility as liberals to help Iranian civil society to grow.

DP: You have said that "[l]iving in Iran is living at the edge and struggling as an intellectual is like walking on a tightrope." Can you explain this?

RJ: The work of an intellectual requires living on the edge. This is the only way the essence of life can be grasped. This is even truer in a challenging country like Iran. Do you remember the epigraph to Somerset Maugham's great novel *The Razor's Edge*, taken from the Upanishads: "The sharp edge of a razor is difficult to pass over; thus the wise say the path to Salvation is hard." I suppose what I am trying to say is that you get used to living with challenges in a society where there is no such thing as a plain and simple life. Life is not easy when you have to live morally in the face of untruth. Maybe intellectuals in Iran have learned to face a life of challenges because the challenge of truth is more crucial to their existence than it is to others. I believe one cannot be a friend of truth without living on the edge. But to do that one has to be gripped by the idea and the passion that life and thought are one. If thinking and aliveness become one for us then certainly we can reach the conclusion that living a challenging life in Iran is a meaningful process. For me as an Iranian philosopher, thinking differently is a form of going beyond the challenges of my daily life in Iran. It's an opening up to the world which goes hand in hand with the act of being free. I think this internal dialogue with oneself—listening to one's inner voice, as Gandhi used to say—but also having an acute sense of the world, could be a quest not only to understand the meaning of our world, but also a ceaseless and restless activity of questioning on the nature of the evil that one has to confront in political life.

In Iran we have grown accustomed to living with political evil but to not thinking about it. I think today more than at any other time our mode of thinking and our mode of judging in Iranian society have a crucial role in determining where Iran can go from here. Thinking democracy and establishing democratic governance in a country like Iran is not an easy task. Unlike what people think, it is more than a simple political enterprise. The challenge here is to focus on the process of democratic consciousness-building which can provide continuity to the political structures of democracy by way of contrast with our authoritarian traditions. This is where philosophical thinking comes to our aid as a grammar of resistance to the tyranny of tradition. This does not mean that I consider the tremendous body of traditions in Iran as mere errors of the past. It means that our political and social traditions are acceptable as long as they enable us to think freely. We may find ourselves at home in our traditions, after all. But we need to distinguish between a false sense of belonging and respect for a common space where the plurality of voices can be realized.

I must admit that I am in fullest sympathy with a mode of thinking that would bring intellectuals into struggle against thoughtlessness and acceptance of things as they are, and speaking and acting by appeal to authority, to tradition or to personal loyalty. Here, I believe, lies the deep paradox between living in and for truth and the commitment to a culture where one can feel at home. Thanks to western traditions of thought, I learned to think philosophically and politically, but I have refused systematically, during the past 30 years of my intellectual life, to abandon the Iranian question as the focal point of my philosophical and political thinking. An independent and critical thinker in Iran who takes responsibility for the marginal status thrust upon him is like an acrobat walking on a tightrope. ∎

Acknowledgements

Chapter 1, "Why So Many Leftists are Flummoxed About Iran," first appeared as "Iran, Solidarity, and the Left" in *Radical Society: A Review of Culture & Politics*, Vol. 30, Nos. 3-4 (2003), an abbreviated version of which appeared as "The Selective Solidarity of the Left" in *In These Times*, November 24, 2003

Chapter 2, "What Iranian Liberalism Can Teach the West," is forthcoming as "Liberalism, Internationalism, and Iran" in Neil Jumonville and Kevin Matson, eds., *Liberalism for a New Century* (University of California Press, 2007)

Chapter 3, "The Necropolitical Imagination: Foucault's Iranian Odyssey Reconsidered," first appeared as "Filling the Void" in *The Common Review* Vol. 4, No. 2 Fall 2005

Chapter 4, "Ideas Whose Time Has Come: A Dialogue With Iranian Philosopher Ramin Jahanbegloo," first appeared in *Logos: A Journal of Modern Society & Culture* Volume 5, Issue 2, Summer 2006

Also available from Prickly Paradigm Press:

continued